'*Qur'ânic Concepts in Islāmic Psychology and Spirituality* is a groundbreaking work that bridges Islamic spirituality and psychology, offering a holistic understanding of human nature through the Qur'ânic lens. With clarity and depth, it explores the alignment of human faculties with fitrah, the transformative power of the five pillars, and key spiritual concepts such as ikhlas (sincerity), sabr (patience) and shukr (gratitude).

This book is an invaluable resource for those seeking to integrate faith with mental and emotional well-being. Rooted in the Qur'an and Hadith, it provides insights that are both accessible and practical, making it an essential guide for personal growth, academic study, and professional practice. A must-read for anyone seeking a deeper understanding of how connecting with Allah leads to psychological resilience.'

Professor Mehmet Ozalp,
Centre for Islamic Studies and Civilisation,
Charles Sturt University

'*In the name of Allāh, the Most Gracious, the Most Merciful.* It is with immense pleasure that I write this endorsement for a book that explores the vital field of Islāmic psychology from a Qur'ânic worldview. The author, Professor Zuleyha Keskin, is the Associate Head of School at CISAC, co-founded ISRA Australia in 2009, leading to the establishment of CISAC at Charles Sturt University, where she played a key role in developing academic programmes, including Islāmic Studies and Islāmic Psychology. Her dedicated contributions to the Muslim community in Australia have earned her the prestigious Order of Australia Medal.

I wholeheartedly endorse *Qur'ânic Concepts in Islāmic Psychology and Spirituality: Application in the Modern World* as a groundbreaking contribution to the field of Islāmic psychology. Professor Zuleyha Keskin masterfully integrates Qur'ānic wisdom with contemporary psychological insights, re-focusing spirituality as the foundation of human well-being. This book challenges secular paradigms by presenting an authentic, faith-based understanding of the human psyche, emphasising the interconnectedness of the *rūḥ* (spirit), *qalb* (heart), *'aql* (intellect), and *nafs* (self). Its structured approach – covering *fiṭrah*, self-purification, and psychological resilience – makes it both practical and deeply transformative. With its strong focus on spiritual well-being, this work fills a critical gap in the field.

This book is an essential resource for students, practitioners, and scholars of psychology, as well as for anyone seeking a deeper understanding of the human psyche and soul from an Islāmic perspective. It offers a much-needed alternative to secular psychological theories, demonstrating that Islāmic psychology is not merely an adaptation of modern psychology, but a complete and independent framework rooted in divine wisdom. I pray that this book serves as a source of guidance and benefit for all who read it, inspiring further exploration, and development in the field. May Allāh reward Professor Zuleyha Keskin for her efforts and grant this work widespread acceptance and impact. Ameen.'

Dr. G. Hussein Rassool,
Professor of Islāmic Psychology

Quranic Concepts in Islamic Psychology and Spirituality

This book explores how the Qur'ân's timeless teachings enrich contemporary psychological theories, bridging the gap between Islamic wisdom and psychological well-being.

It offers a comprehensive guide to understanding and applying Qur'ânic concepts in the realm of mental health. Grounded in Islamic scholarship, it references both classical and modern Islamic sources to explain fundamental Qur'ânic concepts in Islamic psychology. This book is structured around three key areas: first, an Islamic perspective on human faculties, essential for self-knowledge and self-awareness; second, the five pillars of Islam, which play a central role in psychological resilience; and third, various Qur'ânic spiritual concepts linked to mental well-being such as ṣabr (patience), shukr (gratitude), riḍā (contentment), and iṭmi'nān (peacefulness).

By integrating Islamic principles with contemporary psychological insights and promoting a holistic approach to well-being, this book serves as a vital resource for personal development, academic study, and professional practice, particularly for mental health professionals working with Muslim clients.

Zuleyha Keskin is an Associate Professor of Islamic Spirituality and the Course Coordinator of the Graduate Certificate in Islamic Psychology at Charles Sturt University, Australia. She also serves as the Associate Head of School at the Centre for Islamic Studies and Civilisation at Charles Sturt University. Zuleyha is the co-founder of ISRA Academy, the editor-in-chief of the *Australian Journal of Islamic Studies*, and the vice president of the Australian Association of Islamic and Muslim Studies.

Focus Series on Islāmic Psychology and Psychotherapy

Series Editor: Professor Dr. G. Hussein Rassool, Professor of Islāmic Psychology

About the Series

In contemporary times, there is increasing focus on the need to adapt approaches of psychology, counselling psychology and psychotherapy to accommodate the integration of spirituality and psychology. With the increasing focus on the need to meet the wholistic needs of Muslims, there was a call to adapt approaches to the understanding of behaviour and experiences from an Islāmic epistemological and ontological worldview.

The aim of the Focus Series on Islāmic psychology and psychotherapy is to introduce a range of educational, clinical and research interventions relating to Islāmic psychology and psychotherapy that are authentic, practical, concise, and based on cutting-edge research. Each volume focuses on a particular aspect of Islāmic psychology and psychotherapy, its application with a specific client group, a particular methodology or approach, or a critical analysis of existing and emergent theoretical and historical ideas.

Each book in the Focus Series is written, in accessible language, with the assumption that the readers have no prior knowledge of Islāmic psychology and psychotherapy.

Maristāns and Islāmic Psychology
A Historical Model for Modern Implementation
Rania Awaad and Merve Nursoy-Demir

Treating Addiction from an Islāmic Psychology Perspective
By G. Hussein Rassool

Spiritual Integration in Islāmic Psychotherapy: Unveiling the Therapist's Soul
By G. Hussein Rassool

Quranic Concepts in Islamic Psychology and Spirituality: Application in the Modern World
Zuleyha Keskin

Quranic Concepts in Islamic Psychology and Spirituality

Application in the Modern World

Zuleyha Keskin

Routledge
Taylor & Francis Group
LONDON AND NEW YORK

First published 2025
by Routledge
4 Park Square, Milton Park, Abingdon, Oxon OX14 4RN

and by Routledge
605 Third Avenue, New York, NY 10158

Routledge is an imprint of the Taylor & Francis Group, an informa business

British Library Cataloguing-in-Publication Data
A catalogue record for this book is available from the British Library

ISBN: 9781032799353 (hbk)
ISBN: 9781032799384 (pbk)
ISBN: 9781003494614 (ebk)

DOI: 10.4324/9781003494614

Typeset in Times New Roman
by codeMantra

Contents

Preface

Islāmic psychology is deeply rooted in the Qur'ânic worldview, offering a holistic understanding of human nature. It provides a comprehensive view of human nature while also offering clear guidance on how to realise human potential. While modern psychological frameworks often focus on mental and emotional states through the lens of biology or cognitive processes, Islāmic psychology is grounded in the Qur'ân and *ḥadīth*. This foundation supports a holistic approach, integrating spiritual, mental, emotional, physical, and social dimensions to guide human development in a balanced and complete way.

This book has a strong spiritual focus, and this naturally leads to a strong Islāmic psychology focus since Islāmic spirituality and psychology are deeply intertwined. Spirituality is not seen as separate from psychological well-being; rather, the two are interdependent. The state of a person's spiritual life, including their connection with Allāh and their adherence to Divine principles, directly impacts their mental and emotional health. Islāmic psychology provides a framework that goes beyond mental or emotional states; it focuses on all the human faculties as described in the Qur'ân and *ḥadīth*.

The core themes of this book weave together the Qur'ânic perspectives on the human faculties, the core Islāmic practices (the five pillars of Islam), and spiritual concepts that help a believer navigate through life. Collectively, these form the foundation of Islāmic psychology. This book offers a comprehensive understanding of how the Qur'ân addresses the human being for it to thrive in every way, in this life and the afterlife.

Chapter 1 of this book delves into the human faculties as described in the Qur'ân, examining how each of these faculties is designed to fulfil the ultimate purpose of human existence, which is to worship Allāh. The *rūḥ* (spirit), *qalb* (heart), *'aql* (intellect), and *nafs* (self), each serve an important function in fulfilling this ultimate goal. When their nature and function are understood and utilised correctly, humans can then achieve their potential as intended by Allāh.

The chapter begins by exploring the concept of *fiṭrah* (innate nature), which is the natural inclination of every human being towards belief in and worship of Allāh. *Fiṭrah* represents the pure, unaltered state in which humans are born, and while external influences such as upbringing and life experiences can suppress or distort this inclination, the *fiṭrah* remains central to fulfilling one's purpose of creation. The fundamental means to achieve this purpose is to align the human faculties with the *fiṭrah*.

The *rūḥ* is presented as the divine spirit breathed into humans by Allāh, which animates life and provides the capacity to understand and connect with the Creator. It is the source of life, enabling individuals to comprehend the Divine message and mirror Allāh's beautiful names in a limited way, reflecting qualities such as mercy, compassion, and justice. The ultimate purpose of the *rūḥ* is to connect with Allāh.

The *qalb* is described as more than a physical organ; it is a spiritual centre that holds the ability to believe in Allāh and maintain a relationship with Him. The Qur'ân emphasises the importance of purifying the heart to ensure it remains receptive to Divine guidance. A healthy heart leads to spiritual growth, while a diseased heart can block Divine light, leading to moral and spiritual corruption. The ultimate purpose of the *qalb* is to believe in and love Allāh.

The *'aql* is the faculty of reason and understanding, used to know Allāh through contemplation of creation and revelation. It enables reflection on the self, the signs of Allāh in the universe, and the teachings of the Qur'ān. By employing the *'aql* in this manner, a deeper understanding of Allāh's names becomes possible. This then naturally leads to greater knowledge of Allāh. The *'aql* is also crucial for distinguishing right from wrong as well as for making broader ethical decisions. Ultimately, the purpose of the *'aql* is to know Allāh.

Finally, the *nafs*, or self, is presented as the faculty responsible for relating to Allāh, which hinges on the extent to which the *nafs* has been purified. The Qur'ân mentions three different states of the *nafs*: *nafs al-ammārah* (the evil-commanding *nafs*), *nafs al-lawwāmah* (the self-accusing *nafs*), and *nafs al-muṭma'innah* (the *nafs* at peace). The *nafs* must undergo a process of purification to rid itself of egoistic tendencies so that it can be aligned with the *rūḥ* and allow the *fiṭrah* to achieve its purpose. As the *nafs* becomes purified, it allows individuals to better understand themselves in relation to their Creator. Ultimately, the purpose of the *nafs* is to relate to Allāh.

Overall, Chapter 1 outlines how understanding and utilising the human faculties in accordance with the Qur'ânic framework enables individuals to fulfil their ultimate purpose of worshipping Allāh. Each faculty plays a vital role in guiding human behaviour, thought, and spiritual growth, ultimately leading to a harmonious and fulfilling life.

Chapters 2–4 focus on the five pillars of Islām, which are acts of worship that form the foundation of a Muslim's spiritual, mental, physical, and communal life. They contribute to overall well-being through their synergistic effects on different aspects of an individual's life. The five pillars, *Shahādah* (creed), *Ṣalāh* (prayer), *Zakāh* (purifying alms), *Ṣawm* (fasting), and *Ḥajj* (pilgrimage), serve as essential practices designed to nurture a healthy level of detachment from worldly distractions while fostering attachment to Allāh. These acts embody a holistic path that brings believers closer to Allāh, offering numerous mental, physical, and social benefits.

The *Shahādah*, the Islamic creed, represents the central tenet of Islām, which is to acknowledge the oneness of Allāh and accept Muḥammad (pbuh) as His Messenger. The practice of this pillar in everyday life enables believers to detach themselves from false idols such as wealth and status. Such a detachment serves as a reminder of Who is truly worthy of worship, Allāh. More so, the *Shahādah* places Prophet Muḥammad (pbuh) as the role model that the believer aspires to be like, making him the reference point in one's life.

Ṣalāh, the five daily prayers, functions as a spiritual anchor, reminding Muslims of their purpose and relationship with Allāh. It provides structured breaks throughout the day, encouraging believers to momentarily detach from worldly matters and focus on their worship. Beyond spiritual benefits, *Ṣalāh* offers benefits to one's mental and physical well-being, including enhanced discipline, mindfulness, and stress reduction. When performed in congregation, it also strengthens social cohesion within the Muslim community.

Zakāh, the obligatory charity, purifies a Muslim's wealth by redistributing a portion of it to the less fortunate. This act facilitates a healthy detachment from material possessions while fostering empathy and generosity. *Zakāh* serves as a reminder that wealth ultimately belongs to Allāh while promoting social justice by narrowing economic inequalities. It purifies the heart of greed and strengthens the bonds of society through acts of kindness and generosity.

Ṣawm, or fasting, during the month of Ramadan serves to detach individuals from the impulsive desires of their *nafs* that often dictate their actions in daily life. By abstaining from food, drink, and physical needs, believers purify their souls, sharpen their self-discipline, and renew their commitment to Allāh. Fasting also deepens empathy for the less fortunate and encourages gratitude for life's blessings.

Finally, *Ḥajj*, the pilgrimage to Mecca, facilitates a healthy detachment from the sins one commits in this world of desires and distractions by removing the person from their everyday setting where sins are more easily accessible. This healthy detachment from everyday life serves as a reminder of whose commandments should be followed in one's life, Allāh's commandments.

Overall, the five pillars of Islām guide believers towards spiritual, mental, emotional, physical, and social growth, while preparing them for success in the afterlife. Each pillar facilitates a healthy detachment from worldly distractions that could otherwise hinder a true connection with Allāh. The five pillars provide the necessary balance in life for overall well-being.

Chapters 5–8 explore the significance of various Qur'ânic spiritual concepts, highlighting their critical role in Islam as outlined in the Qur'ān and *ḥadīth*. These concepts serve both spiritual and psychological purposes, contributing to a believer's mental well-being and spiritual growth. The essence of these

Qur'ânic concepts is that they encourage believers to develop a deep, conscious connection with Allāh, which in turn facilitates mental and emotional resilience. Whether it is through placing trust in Allāh (*tawakkul*), practicing patience (*ṣabr*), or engaging in reflection (*tafakkur*), these practices guide individuals to navigate life's uncertainties.

Self-awareness and self-regulation are also critical in the Islāmic tradition, ensuring a believer takes responsibility for one's actions while recognising human limitations. Furthermore, practices like repentance (*tawbah*) and seeking forgiveness (*istighfār*) are avenues for emotional healing, allowing individuals to let go of guilt and regret while fostering spiritual and emotional growth. These chapters present Qur'ânic teachings which are integral to achieving psychological well-being by providing a framework that encourages spiritual mindfulness and emotional resilience, which can contribute towards achieving a state of tranquillity. These concepts work together to guide individuals towards a balanced life, grounded in faith, where spiritual and psychological dimensions are deeply interconnected.

Overall, this book seeks to act as a guide for the various Qur'ânic tools available for Muslims to navigate through life in the best possible way.

1 The Human Faculties in the Qur'ân

Introducing the Human Faculties

وَمَا خَلَقْتُ ٱلْجِنَّ وَٱلْإِنسَ إِلَّا لِيَعْبُدُونِ

- *I did not create jinn and humans except to worship Me.*

(Adh-Dhāriyāt 51:56, interpretation of the meaning)

Humanity possesses a multitude of sophisticated faculties, each designed with a distinct function. However, underlying the diversity of these faculties is the singular purpose of worshipping Allāh, as stated in the Qur'ân:

وَمَا خَلَقْتُ ٱلْجِنَّ وَٱلْإِنسَ إِلَّا لِيَعْبُدُونِ

- *I did not create jinn and humans except to worship Me.*

(Adh-Dhāriyāt 51:56, interpretation of the meaning)

This Divine revelation clarifies the fundamental purpose of human creation, leaving no room for doubt as to what the purpose of humankind is. The various faculties serve to facilitate the fulfilment of this fundamental objective, with each faculty contributing towards this singular purpose while also working together.

However, to be able to achieve the full functionality of each faculty, one needs to know their purpose to then be able to utilise them in the best possible way. The human faculties are like different components of a computer. Just as each component of a computer is needed for the complete functioning of the computer, each human faculty is needed to realise the full potential of a human being. Without power, the computer cannot be switched on. Without a keyboard or some type of input, interacting with the computer would not be possible. Without a central processing unit, the data provided to the computer cannot be processed, and so on. Similarly, without the *rūḥ* (spirit), there would be no life in a body, without the physical body, it would not be possible for the spirit to interact with the physical world, and without the *qalb* (heart), *'aql* (intellect), and *nafs* (self), it would not be possible for a person to process

DOI: 10.4324/9781003494614-1

stimuli from their surroundings. However, knowing the existence of these faculties is not enough, even though it is a good starting point. Knowing how these faculties function and utilising them for the purpose they were created is a human responsibility.

A fundamental principle in Islām is for believers to have self-awareness. Without understanding oneself, one cannot know their Creator, and if one does not know their Creator, their primary purpose of existence, worshipping Allāh, will fall short. Otherwise, how does one worship a Being that they do not know? The Qur'ân highlights the important connection between self-awareness and knowledge of Allāh in the verse:

وَلَا تَكُونُوا۟ كَٱلَّذِينَ نَسُوا۟ ٱللَّهَ فَأَنسَىٰهُمْ أَنفُسَهُمْ

- *And do not be like those who forgot Allāh, so He made them forget themselves.*

(Al-Ḥashr, 59:19, interpretation of the meaning)

In this context, the various human faculties mentioned in the Qur'ân will be discussed, namely the *rūḥ* (spirit), *qalb* (heart), *'aql* (intellect), and *nafs* (self). However, before delving into the human faculties, the *fiṭrah* (innate nature) will first be explored. The *fiṭrah* of a person, is their natural state, it is what one is inclined towards. Once the *fiṭrah* is understood, then the role of the faculties in relation to the *fiṭrah* will be appreciated.

Fiṭrah (Innate Nature)

فَأَقِمْ وَجْهَكَ لِلدِّينِ حَنِيفًا ۚ فِطْرَتَ ٱللَّهِ ٱلَّتِى فَطَرَ ٱلنَّاسَ عَلَيْهَا ۚ لَا تَبْدِيلَ لِخَلْقِ ٱللَّهِ
ذَٰلِكَ ٱلدِّينُ ٱلْقَيِّمُ وَلَٰكِنَّ أَكْثَرَ ٱلنَّاسِ لَا يَعْلَمُونَ

- *So, [Prophet] as a man of pure faith, stand firm and true in your devotion to the religion. This is the natural disposition (fitrah) God instilled in mankind - there is no altering God's creation - and this is the right religion, though most people do not realise it.*

(Ar-Rūm, 30:30, interpretation of the meaning)

Allāh has created humankind upon the *fiṭrah*, which means that humankind has an innate inclination or predisposition towards believing in and worshipping Allāh. However, the inclination is not only in relation to belief but also in relation to adherence to the practice of Islām. That is, the *fiṭrah* is "the pristine nature within humans that leads them to acknowledge the truth of God's existence and to follow His guidance" (Utz, 2011, p. 47). The *fiṭrah* is mentioned in a *ḥadīth* where Prophet Muḥammad ﷺ states, "No child is born except that he is upon the *fiṭrah* (innate nature). His parents make him a Jew, or a Christian, or Magian. As an animal delivers a child with limbs intact, do you detect any flaws?" (Muslim (a)). The emphasis in this *ḥadīth* is that human beings are inclined towards Islām, Islām being the "religion of the *Fitrah*" (Rassool, 2021, p. 59). However, this inclination can then be blocked and suppressed, depending on one's upbringing, including all types of external interferences.

This *ḥadīth* has occasionally been translated incorrectly as, "Every child is born a Muslim." However, the hadīth says *fiṭrah*, which means inclined towards faith. In other words, everyone is "born with an intuitive awareness of Divine purpose and a nature built to receive the prophetic message. What remains then is to nurture one's fitra and cultivate this inclination to faith and purity of heart" (Yusuf, 2012, p. 17). It is easy to understand why the *ḥadīth* is sometimes translated as "every child is born a Muslim." The *fiṭrah* is inclined towards the religion, Islām, as mentioned in the Qur'ân.

فِطْرَتَ ٱللَّهِ ٱلَّتِى فَطَرَ ٱلنَّاسَ عَلَيْهَا

- *This is the natural disposition Allāh instilled in humankind.*

(Ar-Rūm, 30:30, interpretation of the meaning)

This means there is an inclination towards being a Muslim. However, there is a difference between inclination, or having the potential, and the actual.

A key aspect of the *fiṭrah* therefore is that human beings are inherently good. A baby is born in a pure form without any sins. Having said that, with the advancement of science, the understanding of this starting point of a newborn has changed. Previously, it would have been believed that every child is born with the same neutralities and inclinations. However, with the advancement of genetic studies and a better awareness about how genes are passed down from parent to child, there is now a realisation that a newborn is predisposed to various states and conditions, influenced by the expression of genes. Some of those states and conditions include illnesses, including mental illnesses, temperament, and character. Furthermore, these states and conditions can be impacted by trauma (Chou et al., 2024). In other words, human beings do not only inherit physical traits but also inherit mental and emotional traits from their parents.

However, this does not take away from the point that a child is born without any sins while also being born with all the tools needed to become an incredible human being. That is, the potential of a newborn is not diminished because of this understanding. While certain traits may predispose one newborn differently from another, advances in the understanding of neuroplasticity have transformed how human development is viewed. Human beings possess immense potential to "re-wire" their brains to overcome challenges and obstacles, whether those challenges and obstacles were inherited genetically or shaped by environmental factors (Peckham, 2023). Basically, a newborn inherently possesses numerous qualities, such as neuroplasticity, to realise its potential while also having human faculties to make this a reality. In this context, "Islāmic psychology emphasises that nothing can erase human *fitrah*, and for those who have buried it, it can be revived" (Haque, 2018, p. 140).

The seed analogy is a powerful way to understand the concept of *fiṭrah*. Each seed contains DNA that has the potential to grow into a beautiful tree. All it needs is the right environment and conditions to express that potential, just as a seed needs fertile soil, water, sunlight, and air. Similarly, humankind is like a seed, with the *fiṭrah* acting as its spiritual DNA. The *fiṭrah* contains all the necessary codes for a person to grow spiritually and realise their potential, becoming like a flourishing tree. The Qur'ân alludes to this inherent capacity when Allāh says,

لَقَدْ خَلَقْنَا ٱلْإِنسَـٰنَ فِىٓ أَحْسَنِ تَقْوِيمٍ

- *Indeed, We created humans in the best form.*

(At-Tīn, 95:4, interpretation of the meaning)

There is inherent excellence and potential within each and every individual. The word *taqwim* (form, composition) used in this Qur'ânic verse hones on the point that the "best ingredients" have been used to create human beings. Some of those ingredients could be understood as the faculties. The seed analogy provides an important insight into the concept of *fiṭrah*. Just as each seed contains the genetic information necessary for it to develop into a tree, so too does every human possess an innate spiritual blueprint, or *fiṭrah*, that guides their development towards a state of excellence. Like a seed needing the right conditions to sprout and grow, humans require a conducive environment to express their *fiṭrah* fully, which includes a nurturing spiritual, physical, emotional, and social environment.

There are incredible benefits to understanding the *fiṭrah*. Firstly, realising one's great potential is a huge starting point for growth. It provides the vision of starting with the end in mind where life's goal is to become a majestic spiritual tree. The power of such a mindset on self-confidence, self-assurance, and self-esteem should never be underestimated. If a person does not believe they have potential, they cannot realise that potential since their beliefs about themself will become a fulfilling prophecy. Whereas if they believe they have what it takes to become a majestic spiritual tree, the drive and the vision is there. What is left is acquiring the knowledge on how to achieve that vision. Secondly, *knowing* the *fiṭrah* is an important starting point for *aligning* with the *fiṭrah*. Such an alignment removes tension and friction between what the *fiṭrah* wants and what the person is. When a person is aligned with their *fiṭrah*, it is like swimming downhill in a stream rather than trying to swim uphill and against the flow. The journey becomes "more natural" and therefore easier as opposed to the struggles of trying to swim uphill against the flow. These opposing scenarios "affect the psychological state of the person and determine relative levels of alignment or misalignment with *fitrah*" (Rothman & Coyle, 2018, p. 1742).

The *fiṭrah* (innate nature) is naturally inclined towards Islām, as stated in the Qur'ân, and Islām provides clear guidance on how to nurture and realise this potential. The Qur'ân and *ḥadīth* give detailed instructions akin to the elements needed to cultivate a tree such as soil, water, air, sunlight, and fertiliser. Islām not only recognises the potential within every human being but also offers precise instructions on how to develop it. A crucial aspect of this development is utilising the human faculties for the very purposes they were created, thereby realising one's spiritual potential. Just as a computer is designed to store, retrieve, and process data, human beings are created to worship Allāh. A computer requires specific components, such as a keyboard, central processing unit, and memory, to fulfil its purpose. Similarly, humans are endowed with faculties like the *rūḥ* (spirit), *qalb* (heart), *'aql* (intellect), and *nafs* (self) to achieve their purpose. Each of these faculties has a distinct function in realising the ultimate goal of worshipping Allāh. If these faculties are not utilised for their intended purposes, they are either underutilised or misused. This leads to dysfunction, comparable to a malfunctioning computer, or results in stunted growth or even deterioration, if the tree analogy is used.

In the next section, each of the four faculties will be examined in detail through the lens of the Qur'ân and *ḥadīth*. This insight will provide a better understanding of their nature, their intended purpose, and how to fulfil that purpose. Before proceeding further, two important disclaimers must be made regarding the discussion of human faculties. Firstly, the four faculties to be explored are metaphysical in nature. Given that humans are bound by the physical world and possess limited knowledge of the metaphysical realm, it is impossible to fully comprehend these faculties. Although the Qur'ân and *ḥadīth* offer valuable insights that allow for an appreciation for these faculties, it is important to acknowledge that this understanding will always be limited. This limitation can be likened to a fish attempting to understand life outside of water; because a fish's existence depends entirely on water, it cannot fully grasp the concept of life beyond it. Similarly, human perception is shaped by experiences in the physical world, which constrains the ability to fully understand the metaphysical. Nevertheless, through the knowledge provided in the Qur'ân and *ḥadīth*, one can still gain a meaningful appreciation of these metaphysical faculties.

The second disclaimer follows naturally from the first. Scholars hold differing opinions regarding the definitions and functionalities of the faculties. This divergence arises because the faculties under discussion are metaphysical entities, which, although experienced, cannot be seen. Consequently, even when referencing the Qur'ân and *ḥadīth*, differences in interpretation are inevitable. This chapter will not explore these varying viewpoints in depth, as this book is neither a theological nor a philosophical text. Instead, the aim is to provide a meaningful appreciation of the faculties for a better understanding of Islāmic psychology and spirituality.

Rūḥ (Spirit)

فَإِذَا سَوَّيْتُهُۥ وَنَفَخْتُ فِيهِ مِن رُّوحِى فَقَعُوا۟ لَهُۥ سَـٰجِدِينَ

- *When I have fashioned him (Adam) and breathed My spirit into him, bow down before him in prostration.*

(Al-Ḥijr, 15:29, interpretation of the meaning)

Purpose of the rūḥ

It is through the *rūḥ* that a person connects with Allāh. In other words, the *rūḥ* inherently seeks to connect with Allāh, as it is "from Allāh." This entity is ultimately what sustains life. It is of such a nature that it is receptive to and capable of comprehending the Divine message. It is also the *rūḥ* that grants the ability and capacity to reflect the names of Allāh, in a limited fashion, thereby enabling a person to realise their full potential.

Rūḥ in the Qur'ân

Rūḥ stems from the triliteral root rā wāw ḥā (ر و ح). This root word occurs in 40 Chapters and appears 57 times in the Qur'ân, in two derived forms. Not all these words refer to the spirit. Other meanings attributed to this root word are wind (e.g., Al Baqarah, 2:164), smell (e.g., Yūsuf, 12:94), and revelation (e.g., Ash-Shūrā, 42:52).

In the context of this chapter, the Qur'ân mentions the *rūḥ* in several verses, often highlighting its creation by Allāh and its role in giving life to the body. Before exploring the nature and purpose of the *rūḥ*, it is crucial to acknowledge that Allāh states in the Qur'ân that only a limited amount of knowledge has been provided about the *rūḥ*.

وَيَسْـَٔلُونَكَ عَنِ ٱلرُّوحِ ۖ قُلِ ٱلرُّوحُ مِنْ أَمْرِ رَبِّى وَمَآ أُوتِيتُم مِّنَ ٱلْعِلْمِ إِلَّا قَلِيلًا

- *[Prophet], they ask you about the spirit (rūḥ). Say, "The spirit (rūḥ) is part of my Lord's domain. You have only been given a little knowledge."*

(Al-Isrā', 17:85, interpretation of the meaning)

Thus, attempting to grasp the *rūḥ* in exhaustive detail is not possible since such detail is not offered in the Qur'ân nor the *ḥadīth*. However, it is possible to gain a certain level of understanding, which will be outlined below.

For instance, the life-giving aspect of the *rūḥ* is clearly mentioned in the following Qur'ânic verse:

ٱللَّ يَتَوَفَّى ٱلْأَنفُسَ حِينَ مَوْتِهَا وَ ٱلَّتِ ى لَمْ تَمُتْ فِى مَنَامِهَا فَيُمْسِكُ ٱلَّتِى قَضَىٰ
عَلَيْهَا ٱلْمَوْتَ وَيُرْسِلُ ٱلْأُخْرَىٰٓ إِلَىٰٓ أَجَل مُّسَمًّى إِنَّ فِى ذَٰلِكَ لَءَايَٰت لِقَوْ م
يَتَفَكَّرُونَ

- *Allāh takes the souls of the dead and the souls of the living while they sleep. He keeps hold of those whose death He has ordained and sends the others back until their appointed time. There truly are signs in this for those who reflect.*

(Az-Zumar, 39:42, interpretation of the meaning)

In this verse, the similarity between death and sleep are highlighted. In both cases, the *rūḥ* is separated from the body. The words of Prophet Muḥammad ﷺ help to better understand this point; "Sleep is the brother of death" (Ṭabarānī, n.d.). In the case of death, the *rūḥ* permanently leaves the body while with sleep, the *rūḥ* returns to the body once a person wakes up. The above Qur'ânic verse can be further explained as follows:

> It is not the human spirit but the human soul that dies. The soul (*nafs*) is, in one respect, the human being itself and, therefore, encompasses the spirit; and in another respect, it is the center or mechanism of worldly life. As for the spirit, it is the source of both bodily and spiritual life. It has an existence independent of the body, and it continues to live after death.
>
> (Unal, 2006, p. 954)

The *rūḥ* is understood as the source of life itself, a divine spark that animates the body. Al-Ghazzālī describes the *rūḥ* as "a subtle body whose source is the cavity of the physical heart, and which spreads by means of the pulsative arteries to all the other parts of the body" (2007, p. 7). Unlike the *nafs*, the *rūḥ* has an existence independent of the body which enables it to exist after death. In contrast, the *nafs* is the aspect of the human being that experiences death, as mentioned in the Qur'ân,

كُلُّ نَفْسٍ ذَآئِقَةُ ٱلْمَوْتِ ۖ ثُمَّ إِلَيْنَا تُرْجَعُونَ

- *Every nafs will taste death. Then to Us will you be returned.*

(Al-ʿAnkabūt, 29:57, interpretation of the meaning)

Thus, while the *nafs* may "die" in the sense of experiencing the end of its life, the *rūḥ* does not. This aligns with the belief in the afterlife in Islām, where the *rūḥ* continues its journey beyond the physical realm into the intermediate realm, and then into the afterlife (*ākhirah*). However, the *rūḥ* has a greater purpose than just keeping a person alive. Since it is from "Allāh's spirit," it has qualities accordingly. Many scholars have understood this to mean that human beings have the capacity to know Allāh like no other creation.

> It is because of this comprehensive making of the human model that man became deserving of Divine vice-regency, and very much capable of absorbing the light which helps him know his Lord and, of course, sustaining his own burning quest on the path of love and longing for Him.
>
> (Ma'arif al-Qur'ân, 15:29–30)

Some scholars interpret this verse to mean that humankind can manifest the qualities or names of Allāh in a limited way. As Maududi explains, the spirit blown into human beings signifies the "Divine characteristics that have been cast on the human body," making humans worthy of being Allāh's vicegerents on earth (Maududi, n.d.). Similarly, scholars like Ibn Arabi, Al-Ghazzālī (1970), and Nursi (2005) have extensively discussed how human beings have the capacity to reflect the names of Allāh in the most comprehensive manner, as humans serve as the most comprehensive mirror to the Divine names.

An incident during the time of Prophet Muḥammad ﷺ explicitly illustrates that humankind can manifest the names of Allāh in a limited fashion: a woman loses her child in a crowd, and she frantically looks for him. One can imagine the mother's distress in such a situation. The mother finally finds her child, after which she compassionately starts to nurse him. Having witnessed this incident, Prophet Muḥammad ﷺ asked his companions, "Do you think this woman can throw her son in the fire?" to which the companions respond, "No." The Prophet then said, "God is more merciful to humankind than this woman is to her son" (Bukhârî (a)). In this incident, Prophet Muḥammad ﷺ is comparing the mercy shown by the mother to Allāh's Mercy in order to highlight the magnitude of Allāh's Mercy. But he does this through comparison, which is the pertinent point here. That is, the mercy shown by the mother is comparable to the mercy shown by Allāh, although a mother's mercy can only be a fraction of the mercy shown by Allāh. This is despite mothers being pinnacles of mercy. There are many hādīth where believers are encouraged to reflect and mirror the names of Allāh. One other such example is:

> Indeed, Allāh is Tayyib (good), and He loves tayyib (what is good); He is Nazif (clean), and He loves cleanliness; He is Karim (kind), and He loves kindness; He is Jawad (generous), and He loves generosity.
>
> (Tirmidhî)

Human beings possess the unique capacity to mirror the names of Allāh like no other creation. They can strive for justice, reflecting the name of Allāh, *Al-'Adl* (The Just). In their pursuit of knowledge and wisdom, they can embody the names *Al-ʿAlīm* (The All-Knowing) and *Al-Ḥakīm* (The Wise). By exercising patience, they mirror *Al-Ṣabūr* (The All-Patient); through forgiveness, they reflect *Al-Ghafūr* (The All-Forgiving); and by expressing gratitude, they embody *Al-Shakūr* (The Appreciative), and so on.

Ultimately, the *rūḥ* is the divine spark that connects humans to Allāh, animating life and enabling the comprehension and reflection of the Divine message. While its full nature remains beyond human understanding, the Qur'ân reveals its vital role in sustaining life and continuing beyond death. Scholars highlight that the *rūḥ* grants humans the unique capacity to mirror the names of Allāh in a limited fashion, embodying qualities like mercy, justice, and wisdom. This ability underscores humanity's special role as Allāh's vicegerents on earth, reflecting the Divine names in their lives. Ultimately, it is through the *rūḥ* that one connects with Allāh.

Qalb (Heart)

أَلَا بِذِكْرِ ٱللَّهِ تَطْمَئِنُّ ٱلْقُلُوبُ

- *Indeed, in the remembrance of Allāh do hearts find rest.*

(Ar-Raʿd, 13:28, interpretation of the meaning)

Purpose of the Heart

The fundamental purpose of the heart is to believe in Allāh. Beyond being a physical organ, the heart serves as a spiritual centre crucial to one's relationship with the Divine. It is the heart that receives the Divine light of belief, provided it has not hardened or been sealed due to misdeeds. If it is kept alive through knowledge and worship, it becomes the location where belief in Allāh is encapsulated. Conversely, it is also the heart that can harbour disbelief, as illustrated in the verse:

مِنَ ٱلَّذِينَ قَالُوٓا۟ ءَامَنَّا بِأَفْوَٰهِهِمْ وَلَمْ تُؤْمِن قُلُوبُهُمْ

- *Those who say, "We believe" with their tongues, but their hearts are in disbelief.*

(Al-Māʾidah, 5:41, interpretation of the meaning)

Heart in the Qur'ân

Qalb stems from the triliteral root qāf lām bā (ب ل ق). This root word occurs in 48 Chapters and appears 168 times in the Qur'ân, in nine derived forms.

While the physical and spiritual hearts are distinct, they are deeply interconnected. In this book, references to the heart pertain to the spiritual heart unless otherwise specified. The central role of the *qalb* and the importance of maintaining its health are emphasised in the Qur'ânic verse:

يَوْمَ لَا يَنفَعُ مَالٌ وَلَا بَنُونَ
إِلَّا مَنْ أَتَى ٱللَّهَ بِقَلْبٍ سَلِيمٍ

- *A day in which neither wealth nor children shall be of any benefit, except one who comes to Allāh with a sound heart.*

(Ash-Shuʿarā', 26:88–89, interpretation of the meaning)

This verse underscores the priority of nurturing the spiritual heart, as it is what truly matters in the sight of Allāh. It also highlights the ultimate insignificance of material wealth and worldly relationships on the Day of Judgement, setting as a reminder the transient nature of worldly possessions and the importance of focusing on the eternal spiritual dimension of life.

Prophet Muḥammad ﷺ also reinforces this point, saying, "Verily, Allāh does not look at your appearance or wealth, but rather He looks at your hearts and actions" (Muslim (b)). This *ḥadīth* highlights the importance of inner qualities and actions over external appearances or material wealth in the eyes of Allāh. It underscores the notion that true worth is measured by the health of one's spiritual heart, which ultimately impacts one's character, intentions, and deeds, rather than one's worth being based on fleeting worldly possessions.

The spiritual heart bears the marks of all the actions a person undertakes throughout their life. Every action leaves an imprint on the heart, influencing its ability, positively or negatively, to fulfil its purpose. For instance, Prophet Muḥammad ﷺ described how sins can stain the heart:

> Verily, when the believer commits a sin, a black spot appears upon his heart. If he repents, abandons the sin, and seeks forgiveness, then his heart will be polished. But if he persists in sin, the blackness increases…
>
> (Ibn Majah)

Thus, the heart is deeply affected by sin, bearing the marks of each transgression. However, just as sins can negatively impact the heart, good actions can have a purifying effect. Acts such as repentance (*tawbah*) and the remembrance of Allāh (*dhikr*) serve as a polish, removing the "dirt" and "stains" that may have accumulated on the heart. The centrality of the heart in the human body is further emphasised through the words of Prophet Muḥammad ﷺ, "Surely there is in the body a small piece of flesh; if it is good, the whole body is good, and if it is corrupted, the whole body is corrupted, and that is surely the heart" (Bukhârî (b)). Without a healthy heart, nothing in the body can function the way it was intended to. While this is the case for the physical heart, it is also the case for the spiritual heart. Just as when the physical heart is not functioning well, it can damage organs, possibly due to a lack of blood supply, so too can the human faculties become dysfunctional due to the spiritual heart not functioning the way it was intended to. In such a case, the *rūḥ* would not be able to connect with Allāh, the *'aql* will not be able to know Allāh, and the *nafs* will not be able to relate to Allāh.

The dangers of having a diseased heart are referred to in numerous parts of the Qur'ân, which impacts one's connection with Allāh as well as one's character, behaviour, thoughts, and emotions (Husain, 2022). Allāh says in the Qur'ân,

فَوَيْلٌ لِّلْقَٰسِيَةِ قُلُوبُهُم مِّن ذِكْرِ ٱللَّهِ ۚ أُو۟لَٰٓئِكَ فِى ضَلَٰلٍ مُّبِينٍ

- *So, woe to those whose hearts are too hard to remember Allāh.*
  (Az-Zumar, 39:22, interpretation of the meaning)

If the heart has become hardened with spiritual diseases, it will not be able to remember Allāh as the Divine light will not be able to enter it. Allāh compares the hard heart to a rock, but goes further and says that hearts can be harder than rocks because even rocks can be a means of providing life through the water that can gush out of them:

ثُمَّ قَسَتْ قُلُوبُكُم منۢ بَعْدِ ذَٰلِكَ فَهِىَ ٱلْحِجَارَةِ أَوْ أَشَدُّ قَسْوَةً وَإِنَّ مِنَ ٱلْحِجَارَةِ
لَمَا يَتَفَجَّرُ مِنْهُ ٱلْأَنْهَٰرُ وَإِنَّ مِنْهَا لَمَا يَشَّقَّقُ فَيَخْرُجُ مِنْهُ ٱلْمَآءُ وَإِنَّ مِنْهَا
لَمَا يَهْبِطُ مِنْ خَشْيَةِ ٱ للَّ وَمَا ٱللَّ بِغَٰفِ ل عَمَّا تَعْمَلُونَ

- *Even after that, your hearts became as hard as rocks, or even harder, for there are rocks from which streams spring out, and some from which water comes when they split open, and others which fall down in awe of Allāh: He is not unaware of what you do.*
  (Al-Baqarah, 2:74, interpretation of the meaning)

But then there are hearts that are receptive of Allāh's Divine light:

أَفَمَن شَرَحَ ٱللَّ صَدْرَ ەُ لِلْسْلَٰمِ فَهُوَ عَلَىٰ نُو ر مِن رَّبِه فَوَيْلٌ لِّلْقَٰسِيَة
قُلُوبُهُم من ذِكْرِ أُو۟لَٰٓئِكَ فِى ضَلَٰل مُّبِين

- *Can (the misguided be like) those whose hearts Allāh has opened to Islām, so they are enlightened by their Lord? So, woe to those whose hearts are hardened at the remembrance of Allāh! It is they who are clearly astray.*
  (Az-Zumar, 39:22, interpretation of the meaning)

An open heart is a believing heart that is receptive to the signs of Allāh, allowing the signs to penetrate the heart so that the knowledge can be internalised. This emphasises the importance of maintaining a healthy and pure heart for one's true nature, their *fiṭrah*, to be able to manifest.

The dangers of a diseased spiritual heart can be further understood by the dangers of a diseased physical heart. For example, a dysfunctional physical heart can result in symptoms such as fatigue, shortness of breath, increased heart rate, and swelling of feet. These can then lead to many organs becoming damaged, resulting in further complications such as kidney failure, muscle wasting, stroke, and ultimately death. Similarly, a diseased spiritual heart impacts the spiritual state of a person, which manifests itself in their thoughts, character, and actions. It is a diseased heart that Satan can have an influence over:

لِيَجْعَلَ مَا يُلْقِى ٱلشَّيْطَٰنُ فِتْنَةً لِ لَّذِينَ فِى قُلُوبِهِم مَّرَضٌ وَ ٱلْقَاسِيَةِ قُلُوبُهُمْ وَإِ ن
ٱلظَّٰلِمِينَ لَفِى شِقَا قٍ بَعِي دٍ

- *He makes Satan's insinuations a temptation only for the sick at heart and those whose hearts are hardened. The evildoers are profoundly opposed [to the Truth].*

(Al-Ḥajj, 22:53, interpretation of the meaning)

A diseased spiritual heart also causes damage to the human faculties, which further exacerbates the spiritual decline of a person. A diseased heart would manifest itself in numerous way such as heedlessness, hypocrisy, pride, arrogance, and vanity (Yusuf, 2012). These diseases can have an immense destructive impact on a person, not only in this life but most importantly, in the afterlife. Ultimately, the diseases of the spiritual heart can cause the "death" of the heart which is disbelief.

لِّيُنذِرَ مَن كَانَ حَيًّا

- *This is a revelation, an illuminating Qur'ân to warn anyone who is truly alive.*

(Yā-Sīn, 36:70, interpretation of the meaning)

What remains is for the believer to strive for a healthy heart. The primary means to maintain a healthy heart is through worshipping Allāh. As Allāh states in the Qur'ân,

وَمَا خَلَقْتُ ٱلْجِنَّ وَٱلْإِنسَ إِلَّا لِيَعْبُدُونِ

- *I did not create jinn and humans except to worship Me.*

(Adh-Dhāriyāt, 51:56, interpretation of the meaning)

Worship involves recognising Allāh as the Creator and fulfilling His commands, such as the pillars of Islām, along with engaging in actions that please Him in daily life. However, true worship is only possible through knowing Allāh, which underscores the importance of the *'aql* (intellect).

'Aql (Intellect)

كَذَٰلِكَ يُبَيِّنُ ٱللَّهُ لَكُمْ ءَايَٰتِهِۦ لَعَلَّكُمْ تَعْقِلُونَ

- *This is how Allāh makes His revelations clear to you, so perhaps you will understand.*

(Al-Baqarah, 2:242, interpretation of the meaning)

Purpose of the 'Aql

The *'aql* is the tool for thinking, with its ultimate purpose being to know Allāh. By utilising the *'aql*, it becomes possible for the believer to understand Allāh through His revelation and creation. The *'aql* also serves as a means to discern between right and wrong, make decisions, and comprehend the world, enabling better life choices. Ultimately, the *'aql* facilitates the realising of one's potential.

'Aql in the Qur'ân

'Aql stems from the triliteral root ʿayn qāf lām (ع ق ل). This root word occurs in 30 Chapters and appears 49 times in the Qur'ân, in one derived form.

'Aql means understanding, perception, sober-mindedness, and prudence. Through the *'aql*, humans perceive things that they cannot perceive through their senses. In this respect, the *'aql* plays a critical role in grasping certain realities such as the existence of Allāh and knowledge of Allāh.

The *'aql* is used to perceive the relationship between cause and effect and between the one who acts and the action itself. For instance, through the use of the *'aql*, one can deduce a speaker by hearing their voice. Also, one can recognise a rose by its scent, even with closed eyes. Similarly, the *'aql* can discern the Creator through the observation of creation. In Arabic, *'aql* is related to the root '*ql*, which essentially means "to bind." Thus, the *'aql* is the faculty that binds humankind to Allāh (Nasr, 1979). A deeper understanding of Allāh is attainable by using the *'aql* for contemplation and introspection. This process involves reflecting on one's own being, the Qur'ân, and the universe.

Through self-reflection, one gains a deeper understanding of their own qualities and needs.

As the Qur'ân states:

أَوَلَمْ يَتَفَكَّرُوا فِىٓ أَنفُسِهِم مَّا خَلَقَ ٱللَّهُ ٱلسَّمَٰوَٰتِ وَٱلْأَرْضَ وَمَا بَيْنَهُمَآ إِلَّا بِٱلْحَقِّ
وَأَجَلٍ مُّسَمًّى

- *Have they not reflected upon their own being? Allāh only created the heavens and the earth and everything in between for a purpose and an appointed term.*

(Ar-Rūm, 30:8, interpretation of the meaning)

This verse highlights the wisdom behind the purpose of creation of the heavens and the earth, and the role of human beings within it. The *'aql* is essential for grasping this purpose.

Moreover, by recognising the finite reflection of Allāh's names within oneself, such as compassion, knowledge, wisdom, and forgiveness, Allāh's names can be comprehended to some extent, names such as the All-Compassionate, All-Knowing, All-Wise, and All-Forgiving. This introspection deepens the understanding of the Creator. Thus, the *'aql* is a critical tool for knowing the self in order to know the Creator.

Reflecting on the Qur'ân using the *'aql* is also of vital importance. The Qur'ân is Allāh speaking to humankind, offering guidance for every aspect of life. Allāh encourages such reflection:

أَفَلَا يَتَدَبَّرُونَ ٱلْقُرْءَانَ ۚ وَلَوْ كَانَ مِنْ عِندِ غَيْرِ ٱللَّهِ لَوَجَدُوا۟ فِيهِ ٱخْتِلَـٰفًا كَثِيرًا

- *Do they not ponder upon the Qur'ân? Had it been from someone other than Allāh, they would have found in it a great deal of discrepancy.*
  (An-Nisā', 4:82, interpretation of the meaning)

Reflecting on the Qur'ân not only provides inspiration and guidance for life, but it also deepens knowledge of Allāh. It provides insight into the names of Allāh, making it a key source for knowing Him through the Qur'ân. The names of Allāh are mentioned frequently in the Qur'ân, helping the reader better understand Him. In this regard, Allāh says,

ۚقُلِ ٱدْعُوا۟ ٱللَّهَ أَوِ ٱدْعُوا۟ ٱلرَّحْمَـٰنَ ۖ أَيًّا مَّا تَدْعُوا۟ فَلَهُ ٱلْأَسْمَآءُ ٱلْحُسْنَىٰ

- *Say, "Call upon Allāh or call upon the Most Merciful. Whichever [name] you call, to Him belong the best names."*
  (Al-Isrā', 17:110, interpretation of the meaning)

Finally, reflecting on the universe deepens one's understanding of the Creator through His creation. Allah encourages His servants to contemplate His countless blessings and the immense power He displays in the creation of the heavens and the earth (Ibn Kathir, n.d.). Allāh encourages such reflection in numerous places in the Qur'ân such as:

وَ ٱخْتِلَٰفِ ٱلَّيْلِ وَ ٱلنَّهَارِ وَمَآ أَنزَلَ ٱللَّ مِنَ ٱلسَّمَآءِ مِن رزْ ق فَأَحْيَا بِهِ ٱلْأَرْضَ بَعْدَ
مَوْتِهَا وَتَصْرِيفِ ٱل رِيَٰح ءَايَٰتٌ لِ قَوْ م يَعْقِلُو ن

- *In the alternation of night and day, in the rain Allāh provides, sending it down from the sky and reviving the dead earth with it, and in His shifting of the winds, there are signs for those who use their reason.*
  (Al-Jāthiyah, 45:5, interpretation of the meaning)

The *'aql* is the faculty or tool needed to identify and understand the Divine names as they are expressed and manifested within the world. It allows the believer to perceive the signs of Allāh in the world and to reflect on their significance. By using reason and intellect, beauty and order can be appreciated, thereby recognising the presence of Allāh's names. For instance, when one observes the cycle of life and death in nature, they can contemplate Allāh's name Al-Muḥyī (The Giver of Life) and Al-Mumīt (The Bringer of Death). Similarly, the order and precision in the universe point to Allāh's name Al-Ḥakīm (The Wise) and Al-Muqtadir (The Powerful Determiner). Then there's the beauty in creation, which reflects the names, Al-Muṣawwir (The Fashioner) and Al-Jamīl (The Beautiful). Thus, when the *'aql* is used for its true purpose and when it is not under the influence of the carnal *nafs*, it can identify the truth as best as humanly possible (Tritton, 1971).

The *'aql* is used not only as a means of knowing the Creator and the creation but also as a tool to make judgements between right and wrong. In this way, believers can discern ethical principles derived from the Qur'ân and Sunnah. The *'aql* guides individuals in making moral decisions in various aspects of life such as in business dealings, relationships, and personal conduct. It helps one to choose actions that are pleasing to Allāh and beneficial to themselves and society. In fact, according to "Islāmic spiritual conceptualisation, a fully developed ʾaql provides rationality, knowledge attainment, appreciation of consequences, and even regulation of emotions" (Khan & Keshavarzi, 2023, p. 198).

Hence, the *'aql* serves as a crucial faculty for understanding and connecting with Allāh, as well as navigating the complexities of life. By employing the *'aql* to reflect on the self, the Qur'ân, and the universe, one can attain a deeper comprehension of Allāh's names and the Divine purpose underlying creation. This intellectual contemplation allows the believer to recognise the manifestations of Allāh's names in the world around them and to appreciate the beauty, order, and wisdom in creation. Furthermore, the *'aql* is indispensable for making sound moral judgements, guiding individuals to align their actions with ethical principles derived from the Qur'ân and Sunnah. Ultimately, when the *'aql* is used for its intended purpose, free from the influences of the *nafs*, it enables deep knowledge of Allāh while living a meaningful, righteous life.

Nafs (Self)

وَنَفْسٍ وَمَا سَوَّىٰهَا
فَأَلْهَمَهَا فُجُورَهَا وَتَقْوَىٰهَا
قَدْ أَفْلَحَ مَن زَكَّىٰهَا
وَقَدْ خَابَ مَن دَسَّىٰهَا

- *By the soul (nafs), and how He formed it, and inspired it [to know] its own rebellion and piety! The one who purifies his soul (nafs) succeeds and the one who corrupts it fails.*

(Ash-Shams, 91:7–10, interpretation of the meaning)

Purpose of the Nafs

The ultimate purpose of the *nafs* is to connect with Allāh. To achieve this, the *nafs* must undergo a journey of purification. In its impure and raw state, it mistakenly claims ownership of certain qualities and abilities. However, as the *nafs* is purified, it comes to realise that Allāh is the true source of these qualities and abilities. Thus, the *nafs* becomes a vital means not only to know Allāh but also to relate to Him.

The Nafs in the Qur'ân

Nafs stems from the triliteral root nūn fā sīn (ن ف س). This root word occurs in 63 Chapters and appears 298 times in the Qur'ân, in four derived forms. The term *nafs* is used in four different meanings in Qur'ân. It has been used to mention species, human being, human physique, and psyche – mind and self (Husain, 2022, p. 79). Husain continues by providing examples of the various ways that *nafs* has been used in the Qur'ân. An example of the usage of *nafs* referring to species is the verse 16:72 which states,

وَٱللَّهُ جَعَلَ لَكُم مِّنْ أَنفُسِكُمْ

- *And Allāh has made for you spouses of your own kind.*

(An-Naḥl, 16:72, interpretation of the meaning)

An example of the usage of *nafs* referring to a human being is the verse 28:33 that states,

قَالَ رَبِّ إِنِّى قَتَلْتُ مِنْهُمْ نَفْسًا فَأَخَافُ أَن يَقْتُلُونِ

- *He said, "O my Rabb, I have killed a person from them, so I fear that they will kill me."*

(Al-Qaṣaṣ, 28:33, interpretation of the meaning)

An example of the usage of *nafs* referring to human physique is the verse 8:72 that states,

إِنَّ ٱلَّذِينَ ءَامَنُوا۟ وَهَاجَرُوا۟ وَجَـٰهَدُوا۟ بِأَمْوَٰلِهِمْ وَأَنفُسِهِمْ

- *Those who believed, emigrated, and strived with their wealth and lives in the cause of Allāh.*

(Al-Anfāl, 8:72, interpretation of the meaning)

While *nafs* has been used with varying meanings in the Qur'ân, this book focuses on the *nafs* in relation to one's connection with Allāh, which hinges on the extent to which the *nafs* (self) has been purified. "The concept of *nafs* holds great significance in Islāmic psychology. It serves as a framework for understanding human behaviour, motivation, and spiritual growth within the context of Islāmic belief and practices" (Rassool & Keskin, 2023, p. 7). This aspect of the *nafs* is highlighted in the following verses:

وَنَفْسٍ وَمَا سَوَّىٰهَا
فَأَلْهَمَهَا فُجُورَهَا وَتَقْوَىٰهَا
قَدْ أَفْلَحَ مَن زَكَّىٰهَا
وَقَدْ خَابَ مَن دَسَّىٰهَا

- *By the soul (nafs), and how He formed it, and inspired it [to know] its own rebellion and piety! The one who purifies his soul (nafs) succeeds and the one who corrupts it fails.*

(Ash-Shams, 91:7–10, interpretation of the meaning)

These verses stress not only the nature of the *nafs* but also the potentiality and duality created within it. It also clearly denotes the possibility of the *nafs* being purified or corrupted (Picken, 2005). In this context, three levels of the *nafs* are mentioned in the Qur'ân.

Nafs al-'ammārah (the evil-commanding *nafs*) is mentioned in the Qur'ān in a quote from Prophet Joseph[1]:

وَمَآ أُبَرِّئُ نَفْسِيٓ ۚ إِنَّ ٱلنَّفْسَ لَأَمَّارَةٌۢ بِٱلسُّوٓءِ إِلَّا مَا رَحِمَ رَبِّيٓ ۚ إِنَّ رَبِّى غَفُورٌ رَّحِيمٌ

- *Yet I do not claim myself free of error, for assuredly the human carnal soul always commands evil, except that my Lord has mercy. Surely my Lord is All-Forgiving, All-Compassionate.*

(Yūsuf, 12:53, interpretation of the meaning)

These words display the awareness of a prophet who knew well that it is not possible to find the right way and be steadfast without the help of Allāh. The evil-commanding *nafs* is known to always command evil. Therefore, it is also known as the tyrannical *nafs* since the "negative tendencies can dominate our lives like an absolute tyrant" (Frager, 1999, p. 3). The main characteristic of this level of the *nafs* is that it is driven by an animalistic desire, with no awareness of spiritual needs. The conscience is also not functional, which means there is no guilt in over-indulgence.

Nafs al-lawwāmah (the self-accusing *nafs*) is mentioned in the Qur'ān as a pledge,

وَلَآ أُقْسِمُ بِٱلنَّفْسِ ٱللَّوَّامَةِ
أَيَحْسَبُ ٱلْإِنسَـٰنُ أَلَّن نَّجْمَعَ عِظَامَهُۥ

- *And I swear by the self-accusing human soul. Does human think that We will never assemble his bones (to resurrect him)?*

(Al-Qiyāmah, 75:2–3, interpretation of the meaning)

This verse reminds the *nafs* that it will need to account for its deeds in the hereafter and therefore should be conscious of its actions. An individual at this level of the *nafs* would be ready to respond to such a warning since there is a sense of responsibility felt. After experiencing an awareness of Allāh and seeing the need to enter a path of spirituality, a person at the level of *al-nafs al-lawwāmah* commits to a way of life in accordance with Islam and tries to control their actions for the better. It is considered the level of awakening since such a person has not mastered their own helm yet, so they stumble along the way. They criticise their self for not being true to their commitments, they learn from their experiences and resolve to a renewed commitment, and so the journey to growth continues.

Nafs al-muṭma'innah (the *nafs* at peace) is the level of the *nafs* at which peace and tranquillity is attained. The Qur'ān mentions this level of the *nafs* as:

يَٰٓأَيَّتُهَا ٱلنَّفْسُ ٱلْمُطْمَئِنَّةُ
ٱرْجِعِىٓ إِلَىٰ رَبِّكِ رَاضِيَةً مَّرْضِيَّةً
فَٱدْخُلِى فِى عِبَٰدِى
وَٱدْخُلِى جَنَّتِى

- *Oh you soul at rest (content). Return to your Lord, well-pleased (with Him), and well-pleasing to Him. Enter, then, among My servants (fully content with servanthood to Me)! And enter my Paradise*!

(Al-Fajr, 89:27–30, interpretation of the meaning)

When *nafs al-muṭma'innah* is reached, the *nafs* is at the station of resignation (*riḍā*). This state of *riḍā* provides a sense of contentment, acceptance, and peace (Keskin, 2021). The purification of the *nafs* is a spiritual journey with the aim of progressing to the higher levels in order for self-actualising to come into fruition (Rassool, 2023).

Ultimately, the *nafs* has been created with an important purpose. Nursi (2005) explains that Allāh has absolutely no limits and one cannot comprehend something that is absolute and unlimited. Since Allāh's names and attributes do not have limits, it is necessary to draw a hypothetical line or imaginary limit for human beings to be able to grasp it to some level. The *nafs* does this. Through life events, the *nafs* experiences pretence dominicality, ownership, power, and knowledge. That is, it places an imaginary limit on the all-encompassing attributes and shares the ownership with Allāh. It is through this process that the *nafs* is used as a measure to understand the names and attributes of Allāh (Nursi, 2005).

How does this "measure" help to understand the names and attributes of Allāh? When apparent ownership is experienced, it leads one to say, "As I made this house and arranged it, so someone must have made the universe and arranged it" (Nursi, 2005, p. 559). Or "Like I am the owner of this house, so too is the Creator the owner of the universe" (Nursi, 2005, p. 559). Similarly, with partial knowledge, one can gain an appreciation for Allāh's infinite knowledge, and with a small amount of acquired art, one may understand the art of the All-Glorious Designer. Thus, the proper use of the *nafs* provides deep insight into the names of Allāh, which are mirrored within the self, leading to knowledge and love of God.

Essentially, the *nafs* is like a mirror, measure, or instrument for seeing or finding. Its real nature is only indicative and indicates the meaning of things other than itself. When the *nafs* understands its role in this way, it abandons its imaginary ownership and consciously transfers true ownership of itself and all other creation to the True Owner. A purified *nafs* is applauded in the Qur'ân:

قَدْ أَفْلَحَ مَن زَكَّـٰهَا

- *Truly he succeeds who purifies it.*

(Ash-Shams, 91:9, interpretation of the meaning)

Such a person has shown their superiority to the angels by properly using the trust of vicegerency committed to them.

On the contrary, if the *nafs* gives power and ownership to itself and the causes surrounding it, it means the *nafs* has not been used for its true purpose. For example, rather than saying "Allāh is the Creator of the heavens and the earth," the nafs at the extreme level says, "I create." Rather than saying "Allāh is the true owner of everything," the nafs says "I am the owner, these are my possessions." The following Qur'ânic verse describes this state since there is a failure to use the *nafs* for its correct purpose.

وَقَدْ خَابَ مَن دَسَّـٰهَا

- *And he fails who corrupts it.*

(Ash-Shams, 91:9, interpretation of the meaning)

In this corrupt state, the universe is not seen in its reality. In such a case, Allāh is completely taken out of the picture; the mirror is no longer seen as the object reflecting the light but is seen as the source of the light, negating the real source of light, which is Allāh.

Therefore, the *nafs* is an important means to relate to Allāh. It helps the believer to know themselves and the creation by comprehending the manifestation of the Allāh's names on the self and the universe. However, as the *nafs* is purified, the true source of those names, Allāh, is recognised while there is a realisation that the creation is merely a mirror reflecting those names in a limited fashion.

Without wanting to put a spanner in the works, but as mentioned previously, there are different opinions about what the *rūḥ* is and what the *nafs* is.

This is applicable to the *qalb* and *'aql* as well. For example, Ibn Abi al-Izz states,

> As for the question whether soul (*nafs*) and spirit (*rooh*) are two different things or the same thing, the correct view is that the words mean different things, some of which are the same and some that differ. Take for instance *nafs*. Sometimes it refers to something that is associated with the body. Hence when we want to refer to something isolated from the body, we use the term *rooh*. Thirdly, *nafs* may mean blood… As for *rooh*, it does not refer to the body, neither by itself nor in combination with *nafs*.
>
> (Ibn Abi al-Izz as cited in Zarabozo, 2002, pp. 59–60)

It is important to be aware of the differing opinions about how each faculty is defined and how they relate to each other. Despite the differing views, the general purpose of each faculty in the human body can be appreciated.

Conclusion

The *fiṭrah* (innate nature) of a human being was explored after which the main human faculties, as mentioned in the Qur'ân, were discussed, namely the *rūḥ* (spirit), *qalb* (heart), *'aql* (intellect), and *nafs* (self). The ultimate purpose of the faculties is to facilitate the worship of Allāh, as stated in the Qur'ân. Each faculty has a distinct function and contributes to the fulfilment of this purpose in its own way. The *fiṭrah*, or innate nature, is the spiritual DNA of a person. It inclines individuals towards believing in and adhering to the religion of Islām. Although every child is born with this inclination, it can be suppressed or influenced by external factors. Understanding the *fiṭrah* is important for aligning oneself with it and removing tension and friction between what the *fiṭrah* wants and what one is. Understanding the *fiṭrah* also means knowing one's potential, which facilitates the realising of one's potential.

The *rūḥ*, or spirit, is a means to connect with Allāh. It is the source of life and gives humans the capacity to comprehend and mirror the names of Allāh. Also, the Qur'ân mentions the *rūḥ* in several verses, emphasising its role in giving life to the body and its ability to interact with the physical and spiritual worlds.

The *qalb*, or heart, is not just a physical organ but also a spiritual centre. Its fundamental purpose is to believe in Allāh and maintain a healthy relationship with the Divine. A diseased heart can lead to spiritual and moral corruption, while a purified heart can find rest and contentment in the remembrance of Allāh.

The *'aql*, or intellect, is the tool for thinking and understanding. It enables humans to know Allāh through His revelation and creation. By reflecting on oneself, the Qur'ân, and the universe, one can attain a deeper understanding of Allāh. The *'aql* also helps individuals make ethical decisions and discern right from wrong.

The *nafs*, or self, facilitates a person to relate to Allāh. It goes through a journey of purification, realising that Allāh is the true source of its qualities and abilities. The Qur'ân mentions three levels of the *nafs*: the evil-commanding *nafs*, the self-accusing *nafs*, and the *nafs* at peace. Purifying the *nafs* allows individuals to know themselves, the creation, and Allāh.

Note

1 There are many exegetes who say this expression comes from the wife of Potiphar (Zalikha or Zuleykha). Either way, it does not take away from the way the Qur'ān describes the *nafs* at this level.

References

Bukhârî (a). In book reference: Book 78, Hadith 30. English translation: Vol. 8, Book 73, Hadith 28. https://sunnah.com/bukhari:5999.

Bukhârî (b). In book reference: Book 2, Hadith 45. English translation: Vol. 1, Book 2, Hadith 50. https://sunnah.com/bukhari:52.

Chou, P. C., Huang, Y. C., & Yu, S. (2024). Mechanisms of epigenetic inheritance in post-traumatic stress disorder. *Life*, *14*(1), 1–12. https://doi.org/10.3390/life14010098.

Frager, R. (1999). *Heart, self, and soul: The Sufi psychology of growth, balance, and harmony*. Quest Books.

Ghazzālī, A. H. (1970). *Ninety-nine names of God in Islam* (R. C. Stade, Trans.). Daystar Press.

Ghazzālī, A. H. (2007). *Wonders of the heart* (W. J. Skellie, Trans.). Islamic Book Trust.

Haque, A. (2018). Psychology from an Islamic perspective. In S. Fernando & R. Moodley (Eds.), *Global psychologies: Mental health and the global south* (pp. 137–150). Palgrave Macmillan.

Husain, W. (2022). It's time to translate the quranic words, nafs & qalb as referring to mind & intelligence. *Islamiyyat, 44*(2), 77–95. https://doi.org/10.17576/islamiyyat-2022-4402-06/.

Ibn Majah. Sunan Ibn Majah 4244. In-book reference: Book 37, Hadith 145. English translation: Vol. 5, Book 37, Hadith 4244. Grade: Hasan (Darussalam). https://sunnah.com/ibnmajah:4244.

Keskin, Z. (2021). *Attaining inner peace in Islam*. Springer.

Khan, F., & Keshavarzi, H. (2023). Theoretical foundations and clinical applications of traditional Islamically integrated psychotherapy. In P. S. Richards, G. E. K. Allen, & D. K. Judd (Eds.), *Handbook of spiritually integrated psychotherapies* (pp. 193–212). American Psychological Association. https://doi.org/10.1037/0000338-010.

Ma'arif Al-Qur'an. (n.d.). *Quran.com.* Retrieved from https://quran.com/en/15:29/tafsirs/en-tafsir-maarif-ul-quran (accessed 9 September 2024).

Maududi, S. A. A. (n.d.). *Tafhim al-Qur'an - The Meaning of the Qur'an*. https://www.englishtafsir.com/Quran/15/index.html#sdfootnote19sym (accessed 9 September 2024).

Muslim (a). In-book reference: Book 45, Hadith 42. English translation: Book 32, Hadith 6221. https://sunnah.com/muslim:2659a.

Muslim (b). In-book reference: Book 46, Hadith 40. English translation: Book 33, Hadith 6429. https://sunnah.com/muslim:2564c.

Nasr, S. H. (1979). Intellect and intuition: Their relationship from the Islamic perspective. *Studies in Comparative Religion, 13*(1), 1–9.

Nursi, S. (2005). *The words* (H. Akarsu, Trans.). The Light Inc.

Peckham, H. (2023). Introducing the Neuroplastic Narrative: A non-pathologizing biological foundation for trauma-informed and adverse childhood experience aware approaches. *Frontiers in Psychiatry, 14*, 1–20. https://10.3389/fpsyt.2023.1103718.

Picken, G. (2005). Tazkiyat al-nafs: The Qur'anic Paradigm. *Journal of Qur'anic Studies*, *7*(2), 101–127.

Rassool, G. H. (2021). *Islamic psychology: Human behaviour and experience from an Islamic perspective*. Routledge. https://doi.org/10.4324/9780429354762.

Rassool, G. H. (2023). *Islāmic psychology: The basics*. Routledge. https://doi.org/10.4324/9781003312956.

Rassool, G. H., & Keskin, Z. (2023). Positioning the self (nafs) in Islāmic psycho-spirituality. *Journal of Spirituality in Mental Health, 27*(1), 1–10. https://doi.org/10.1080/19349637.2023.2264848.

Rothman, A., & Coyle, A. (2018). Toward a framework for Islamic psychology and psychotherapy: An Islamic model of the soul. *Journal of Religion and Health, 57*, 1731–1744. https://doi.org/10.1007/s10943-018-0651-x.

Ṭabarānī. (n.d.). al-Mu'jam al-Awsaṭ lil Ṭabarānī [Middle encyclopaedia of Hadith transmitters by Tabarani]. *Daily Hadith Online*. https://www.abuaminaelias.com/dailyhadithonline/2016/03/24/people-jannah-not-sleep-die/ (accessed 9 September 2024).

Tafsir Ibn Kathir. (n.d.). *Quran 45:5 - Tafsir Ibn Kathir*. Quran.com. Retrieved from https://quran.com/45:5/tafsirs/en-tafisr-ibn-kathir (accessed 9 September 2024).

Tirmidhî. In-book reference: Book 43, Hadith 72. English translation: Vol. 5, Book 41, Hadith 2799. https://sunnah.com/tirmidhi:2799.

Tritton, A. S. (1971). Man, nafs, rūḥ, 'aql. *Bulletin of the School of Oriental and African Studies*, *34*(3), 491–495.

Unal, Ali. (2006). *The Qur'an with annotated interpretation in modern English*. The Light Inc.

Utz, A. (2011). *Psychology from the Islamic perspective.* International Islamic Publishing House.

Yusuf, H. (2012). *Purification of the heart: Signs, symptoms, and cures of the spiritual diseases of the heart.* Dar Al Taqwa.

Zarabozo, J. (2002). *Purification of the soul: Concept, process and means*. Al-Basheer Publications & Translations.

2 The Five Pillars

Introduction and Qur'ânic Practice of *Shahādah*

Introduction: The Five Pillars: Qur'ânic Practices

Allāh's Messenger ﷺ said: Islām is based on (the following) five (pillars):

1 To testify that none has the right to be worshipped but Allāh and Muḥammad ﷺ is Allāh's Messenger.
2 To offer the prayers (*Ṣalāh*) dutifully and perfectly.
3 To pay *Zakāh* (i.e., obligatory charity).
4 To perform *Ḥajj* (i.e., pilgrimage to Mecca).
5 To observe fast during the month of Ramaḍān.

The five pillars of Islām are fundamental acts of worship that provide a framework for a Muslim's faith and practice. They are considered foundational to Islām, much like pillars are to a building. Each pillar plays a crucial role in developing one's relationship with Allāh and to fulfil one's purpose in life as a believer. Like the pillars of a building, each pillar of Islām is essential, and neglecting any one of them can weaken the overall structure of a believer's faith. Embracing these pillars strengthens one's connection to their religion, providing guidance for living a righteous life and ultimately leading to spiritual fulfilment that emanates as inner peace. This chapter will provide an introductory explanation to the spiritual significance of each pillar after which it will delve into the first pillar of Islām, the *Shahādah*. Chapter 3 will focus on *Ṣalāh* and *Zakāh*, while Chapter 4 will focus on *Ṣawm* and *Ḥajj*.

Three Aspects to the Five Pillars

The five pillars of Islām are life-changing acts of worship, each serving as a multi-dimensional spiritual practice with deep significance for the practitioner. The pillars offer more than just a path to the afterlife; they are also integral to shaping a fulfilling life in the present. They have a transformative effect, akin to a spring that nourishes and revitalises the soul, leading to spiritual growth that is

DOI: 10.4324/9781003494614-2

otherwise unattainable. With such spiritual growth comes peace and serenity as the believer feels closer to their Creator. Hence, by engaging in the five pillars, believers solidify their faith while also fostering a strong connection with Allāh and their fellow believers. This grounding offers stability and purpose, aligning them with their *fiṭrah*, their innate nature, and ensuring that their faculties are used for the purposes they were created for. In doing so, believers are guided towards fulfilling their life's purpose according to Islāmic teachings.

Moreover, the practice of the five pillars serves to transform individuals into more spiritual beings. Through the ongoing declaration and witnessing of the oneness of Allāh, regular prayer, fasting, charity, and pilgrimage, Muslims purify their heart and *nafs* while cultivating virtues such as patience, humility, gratitude, and compassion. These virtues not only benefit the individual's spiritual well-being but also enhance their interactions with others and their contribution to society.

Furthermore, extensive research has shown that the practice of the five pillars of Islām have a significantly positive impact on the mental well-being of the practitioner (Husain, 1998; Abdel-Khalek & Lester, 2012; Turner, 2015). The holistic framework of these practices fosters a sense of purpose, community, and inner peace. Regular observance of these pillars also instils discipline, promotes mindfulness, and facilitates taking command of one's life. These practices collectively contribute to lower stress levels, improved emotional regulation, and greater resilience in facing life's challenges (Najam et al., 2019). The emphasis on regular reflection and connection with a higher power, Allāh, provides a stable foundation for mental and emotional stability (Yucel, 2024).

Moreover, the communal aspects of these practices enhance social support networks, reducing feelings of isolation and increasing a sense of connectedness with others (Abolfathi Momtaz et al., 2011). This combination of spiritual devotion, community involvement, and personal discipline creates a supportive environment that nurtures an overall well-being and fosters a balanced and fulfilling life.

Overall, the five pillars of Islām offer a comprehensive approach to spiritual development by facilitating a connection with Allāh, which positively impacts every facet of a believer's life. They provide a roadmap for living a life of meaning and fulfilment.

Each pillar has three aspects to them that helps to achieve the above-mentioned:

- Aspect looking to Allāh
- Fundamental spiritual benefit for the practitioner
- Other spiritual, social, mental, and physical benefits

Aspect Looking to Allāh

Just as Allāh created the universe and everything within it, Allāh has also prescribed the rituals that define Islām. The five pillars are meticulously designed by the Creator, who knows His creation, including human beings, better than anyone or anything else. Therefore, Allāh knows precisely what is needed for humans to thrive and fulfil their purpose on this earth.

With these practices, Allāh is primarily looking for the devotional and spiritual meaning that they convey.

لَن يَنَالَ ٱللَّهَ لُحُومُهَا وَلَا دِمَآؤُهَا وَلَـٰكِن يَنَالُهُ ٱلتَّقْوَىٰ مِنكُمْ

- *(Bear in mind that) neither their flesh nor their blood reaches Allāh, but only piety and consciousness of Allāh reach Him from you...*

(Al-Ḥajj, 22:37,
interpretation of the meaning)

That is, with each practice, there is a message, a meaning that is being expressed from the creation towards the Creator. In other words, they are much more than blindly performed rituals, they express great meanings through their performance in the sight of Allāh. Furthermore, there is a close relationship between the outward form of the rituals performed and spiritual meaning that underpins these practices. The spiritual meaning is what ascends to Allāh, and the actions become the vessels that convey them.

مَن كَانَ يُرِيدُ ٱلْعِزَّةَ فَلِلَّهِ ٱلْعِزَّةُ جَمِيعًا إِلَيْهِ يَصْعَدُ ٱلْكَلِمُ ٱلطَّيِّبُ وَٱلْعَمَلُ ٱلصَّـٰلِحُ
يَرْفَعُهُ

- *Whoever desires might, and glory should know that all might, and glory belong to Allāh alone. To Him ascends all good words, and He exalts the good deed...*

(Fāṭir, 35:10,
interpretation of the meaning)

These practices go beyond the physical realm; they blossom in the metaphysical realm as they ascend to the heavens. The metaphysical world includes this life but it also transcends it as it has far-reaching abilities to the afterlife as well.

To better understand how these practices serve as vessels conveying greater meaning than the acts themselves, consider a book as an example. A book exists physically, with words arranged across its pages. If a book is perceived solely as a physical object, it would appear as a collection of pages with words printed on them. However, a book is much more than its physical form. Each book is like a world, conveying meaning through the arrangement of words in a specific order that transcends the individual words. This is made possible by the book serving as a vessel, a medium, through which the words are conveyed. Put differently, if the book is not used as a vessel, it is not possible to convey the meanings desired by the author. The role of the vessel cannot be underestimated. Allāh alludes to the power of words and acts bound by this physical world in the following Qur'ânic verse:

أَلَمْ تَرَ كَيْفَ ضَرَبَ ا للُّ مَثَلً كَلِمَةً طَيِّبَةً كَشَجَرَةٍ طَيِّبَةٍ أَصْلُهَا ثَابِت
وَفَرْعُهَا فِى ٱلسَّمَآءِ
مْ يَتَذَكَّرُو ن تُؤْتِىٓ أُكُلَهَا كُلَّ حِينِۭ بِإِذْنِ رَبِّ هَا وَيَضْرِبُ ا للُّ ٱلْأَمْثَالَ لِلنَّاسِ لَعَلَّهُمْ يَتَذَكَّرُو ن
وَمَثَلُ كَلِمَةٍ خَبِيثَةٍ كَشَجَرَةٍ خَبِيثَةٍ ٱجْتُثَّتْ مِن فَوْقِ ٱلْأَرْضِ مَا لَهَا مِن قَرَارٍ

- *[Prophet], do you not see how Allāh makes comparisons? A good word is like a good tree whose root is firm and whose branches are high in the sky, yielding constant fruit by its Lord's leave. Allāh makes such comparisons for people so that they may reflect. But an evil word is like a rotten tree, uprooted from the surface of the earth, with no power to endure.*

(Ibrāhīm, 14:24–26,
interpretation of the meaning)

Similarly, every act of worship is like a good tree. It has a spiritual existence, branching into the heavens to yield fruits in every worldly and otherworldly season. Each act of worship manifests its fruits, which are witnessed and appreciated by Allāh.

وَمَن يَقْتَرِفْ حَسَنَةً نَّزِدْ لَهُۥ فِيهَا حُسْنًا ۚ إِنَّ ٱللَّهَ غَفُورٌ شَكُورٌ

- *If anyone does good, We shall increase it for him. Allāh is most forgiving and most appreciative.*

(Ash-Shuʿarāʾ, 42:23,
interpretation of the meaning)

In this sense, the actions undertaken within the five pillars are primarily spiritual, transcending the mere physical realm. While the physical acts are essential for manifesting this spiritual essence in the outer world, they are not the ultimate goal in themselves. Instead, they serve as a means to express and embody the deeper spiritual meanings inherent in these practices. It is the spiritual meaning of these acts which are significant for Allāh:

وَلَـٰكِن يَنَالُهُ ٱلتَّقْوَىٰ مِنكُمْ

- *But only piety and consciousness of Allāh reach Him from you.*

(Al-Ḥajj, 22:37,
interpretation of the meaning)

Therefore, the physical acts of the five pillars cannot be separated from the spiritual meaning they portray since the rituals are the vessels. Without the vessel, there is no means of relaying the message. The vessel ensures the spiritual meaning is expressed.

Fundamental Spiritual Benefit of Each Pillar

Each pillar of Islām offers a distinct spiritual benefit that contributes to the practitioner's spiritual growth and closeness to Allāh. These benefits are rooted in the concept of detachment, which involves freeing oneself from worldly distractions that hinder the spiritual connection with the Divine. However, this detachment does not advocate for a complete renunciation of the world; rather, it promotes a balanced approach that allows the believer to navigate the material world while maintaining a strong spiritual bond with Allāh.

This concept of detachment is about finding a balance between worldly attachments and spiritual growth. It is about recognising the temporary nature of worldly pleasures and striving for a deeper, lasting connection with the Divine. By practicing a healthy level of detachment from the world through the pillars of Islām, believers can maintain a healthy balance between their spiritual and worldly obligations, ensuring that they can function effectively in the world while nurturing their spiritual well-being.

The next section discusses how each pillar of Islām facilitates this healthy detachment. Then, there will be a detailed explanation of how each pillar of Islām benefits the practitioner in fulfilling a more enriching life, spiritually, mentally, emotionally, socially, and physically.

Shahada (Creed)

The practitioner witnesses and testifies that there is no deity but Allāh and that Muḥammad ﷺ is the Messenger of Allāh. Through this act of witnessing and testifying, the person detaches themselves from false gods, which can otherwise become a barrier between the believer and Allāh. The false gods can take shape in different forms such as wealth, beauty, status, health, and children. When these attachments become the source of one's purpose, value, security, and happiness in an unhealthy way, they are replacing Allāh as the true God. By practicing the *Shahādah*, it enables a healthy detachment from these worldly attachments. Such a detachment serves as a reminder of Who is truly worthy of worship, Allāh. Moreso, the *Shahādah* places Prophet Muḥammad ﷺ as the role model that the practitioner aspires to be like, making him the reference point in one's life.

Ṣalāh *(Five Daily Prayers)*

The practitioner observes the five daily prayers at prescribed times, which fosters a healthy detachment from worldly matters, at set times, that might otherwise divert them from their true purpose. Daily life can easily engulf the individual, leading to a state of forgetfulness about one's essential reason for existence, which can then result in making worldly success the primary focus of one's day. This healthy detachment from the world serves as a reminder of who should be at the centre of a believer's life, Allāh.

Ṣawm *(Fasting)*

Fasting during the month of Ramaḍān entails abstaining from food, drink, and other physical needs from dawn to sunset. This practice serves to detach individuals from the impulsive desires of their *nafs* that often dictate their actions in daily life. By refraining from fulfilling these basic needs, individuals learn to control their desires and impulses, allowing their higher, more reflective selves to guide their behaviour. This healthy detachment from physical desires serves as a reminder of what a believer's primary drive should be; to seek the pleasure of Allāh.

Zakāh *(Purifying Alms)*

The act of giving a portion of one's wealth to those in need, known as *Zakāh*, serves to cultivate a healthy detachment from material possessions. Wealth, if unchecked, can easily become a dominant force in one's life, shaping one's goals and priorities, whereby the accumulation of wealth becomes the driving force in one's life. The act of charity helps break the hold that wealth can have on the spiritual heart, which could otherwise cause its spiritual decay. This healthy detachment from wealth serves as a reminder of who the true owner of wealth is, Allāh.

Ḥajj *(Pilgrimage)*

The pilgrimage to the holy city of Mecca is a once in a lifetime practice, which transforms the way life and the self is perceived. *Ḥajj* is a healthy detachment from the sins one commits in this world of desires and distractions by removing the person from their everyday setting. By removing a person from their usual environment, it becomes an opportunity for the practitioner to reset their life to a life which is distant from sins, sins that would otherwise take hold of them. This healthy detachment from one's everyday life serves as a reminder of whose commandments should be followed in one's life, Allāh's commandments.

***Shahādah* (Creed)**

هُوَ ٱللَّهُ ٱلَّذِى لَآ إِلَـٰهَ إِلَّا هُوَ

- *He is Allāh, there is no god other than Him.*

(Al-Ḥashr, 59:22,
interpretation of the meaning)

مُّحَمَّدٌ رَّسُولُ ٱللَّهِ

- *Muḥammad is the messenger of Allāh.*

(Al-Fatḥ, 48:29,
interpretation of the meaning)

The *Shahādah* is to proclaim, "I bear witness that there is no god but Allāh and I bear witness that Muḥammad is the Messenger of Allāh." The act of bearing witness to Allāh's unity is the most fundamental act of a Muslim being the entry point into the religion of Islām. However, not only is it an entry point, but it is also a testimony that assumes the acceptance of what the S*hahādah* entails; the belief in the words of Allāh, the Qur'ân, which was revealed to Prophet Muḥammad ﷺ. This then leads to a way of life, which is in line with the teachings of the Qur'ân and Prophet Muḥammad's ﷺ Sunnah. In other words, the *Shahādah* is the practice upon which all other Islāmic beliefs and practices depend (Murata & Chittick, 2015).

Thus, the *Shahādah* is more than uttering words. It is to witness the existence of Allāh every day as the believer makes their way through life. The word *shahādah* literally means "to testify" or "to bear witness." A Muslim testifies that Allāh is the only deity, not only with the heart and mind but also with every cell of their body. At this point, there is absolute conviction and belief in Tawhîd, the oneness of Allāh.

إِنَّمَا ٱلْمُؤْمِنُونَ ٱلَّذِينَ ءَامَنُوا۟ بِٱللَّهِ وَرَسُولِهِۦ ثُمَّ لَمْ يَرْتَابُوا۟ وَجَـٰهَدُوا۟ بِأَمْوَٰلِهِمْ وَأَنفُسِهِمْ
فِى سَبِيلِ ٱللَّهِ ۚ أُو۟لَـٰٓئِكَ هُمُ ٱلصَّـٰدِقُونَ

- *The true believers are the ones who have faith in Allāh and His Messenger and leave all doubt behind, the ones who have struggled with their possessions and their persons in God's way: they are the ones who are true.*

(Al-Ḥujurāt, 49:15,
interpretation of the meaning)

To bear witness that Allāh is the only deity is made possible through reflection and pondering. Hence, there must be conviction in what is uttered for it to be sincere. The uttering of the *Shahādah* is not only the result of what is read or witnessed in the Qur'ân but also what is witnessed in creation. The Qur'ân uses the word *ayāh* (signs) to refer to the actual verses of the Qur'ân as well as the signs Allāh has placed in the natural world for the reflecting human heart and mind:

وَهُوَ ٱلَّذِى مَد لأَرْض وَجَعَلَ فِيهَا رَوَٰسِىَ وَأَنْهَٰرًا وَمِن كُ ل ٱلثَّمَرَٰتِ جَعَلَ فِيهَا
زَوْجَيْنِ ٱثْنَيْنِ يُغْشِى ٱلَّيْلَ ٱلنَّهَارَ إِن فِىذَٰلِ كلَٰيَٰتٍ لِقَوْمٍ يَتَفَكَّرُونَ

- *And it is He who spread out the earth and set thereon mountains standing firm and (flowing) rivers: and fruit of every kind He made in pairs: He draws the night as a veil over the Day. Behold, verily in these things there are signs (ayāh) for those who think and reflect.*

(Ar-Raʿd, 13:3,
interpretation of the meaning)

The Qur'ân is the word of Allāh, filled with signs affirming His existence and oneness. Similarly, the universe is Allāh's creation, equally rich with signs of His existence and oneness. The natural world, particularly the earth with its diverse inhabitants and environments, is where the Divine creativity of Allāh is most vividly displayed and witnessed by humankind. This makes the earth a rich reflection of Allāh's names and an essential source of knowledge that deepens belief in Allāh (Keskin & Ozalp, 2020).

The second part of the *Shahādah*, testifying that Muḥammad ﷺ is the messenger of Allāh, is an essential component of the testimony. It acknowledges that Muḥammad ﷺ is the final messenger of Allāh to whom the Qur'ân was revealed. One cannot complete the *Shahādah* without this belief, for it was to Prophet Muḥammad ﷺ that the Qur'ân was revealed. Therefore, the belief in the Qur'ân as the word of Allāh can only hold if one believes in Muḥammad ﷺ as the last messenger.

Furthermore, while the Qur'ân is the word of Allāh, Prophet Muḥammad ﷺ is the role model or the human template who brought the Qur'ân to life. Hence, the *Shahādah* can only be fully practiced when the Sunnah of Prophet Muḥammad ﷺ is followed. Allāh gives clear instructions in the Qur'ân to follow the way of Prophet Muḥammad ﷺ:

يَـٰٓأَيُّهَا ٱلَّذِينَ ءَامَنُوٓا۟ أَطِيعُوا۟ ٱللَّهَ وَأَطِيعُوا۟ ٱلرَّسُولَ

- *Oh, you who believe! Obey Allāh and obey the Messenger…*

(An-Nisāʾ, 4:59,
interpretation of the meaning)

Not only is the Sunnah the interpretation of the Qur'ân, but it is also the practical exegesis of the Qur'ân, as well the application of Islām in the most ideal way (Al-Qaradawi, 2007). In other words, it is Islām embodied in life. Following the way of the Sunnah is so important that Allāh says in the Qur'ân,

قُلْ إِن كُنتُمْ تُحِبُّونَ ٱللَّهَ فَٱتَّبِعُونِى يُحْبِبْكُمُ ٱللَّهُ وَيَغْفِرْ لَكُمْ ذُنُوبَكُمْ ۗ وَٱللَّهُ غَفُورٌ رَّحِيمٌ

- *Say (to them, O Messenger): 'If you indeed love Allāh, then follow me, so that Allāh will love you and forgive you your sins. Allāh is All- Forgiving, All-Compassionate'.*

(Āl ʿImrān, 3:31,
interpretation of the meaning)

The connection between following Prophet Muḥammad ﷺ and loving Allāh is explicitly stated in this verse. Allāh cannot truly be loved if Prophet Muḥammad's ﷺ way, the Sunnah, is not followed. The second part of the *Shahādah* reinforces this important point.

Shahādah as an Act of Worship

The *Shahādah*, as an act of worship, is not only an acknowledgement made with the heart and mind but also a declaration that forms the foundation upon which a believer builds their life.

This acknowledgement arises from the deep conviction that Allāh is the sole creator of the universe and everything it encompasses. Every aspect of creation, from the vastness of the cosmos to the intricacies of life, is a testament to Allāh's omnipotence and wisdom. The universe was not brought into existence without a profound purpose, as the Qur'ân clearly states,

وَمَا خَلَقْنَا ٱلسَّمَآءَ وَٱلْأَرْضَ وَمَا بَيْنَهُمَا لَـٰعِبِينَ

- *We did not create the heavens and the earth and everything in between for sport.*

(Al-Anbiyāʾ, 21:16,
interpretation of the meaning)

This verse underscores the intentionality behind creation, dismissing any notion that the universe is a product of chance or play. Moreover, Allāh challenges humanity to reflect on their own existence with a rhetorical question in the Qur'ân:

أَفَحَسِبْتُمْ أَنَّمَا خَلَقْنَـٰكُمْ عَبَثًا وَأَنَّكُمْ إِلَيْنَا لَا تُرْجَعُونَ

- *Did you then think that We had created you without purpose, and that you would never be returned to Us?*

(Al-Muʾminūn, 23:115,
interpretation of the meaning)

This question serves as a reminder that human life, like the universe, is imbued with purpose. It calls believers to recognise that their existence is not arbitrary but is part of a Divine plan, with ultimate accountability and a return to Allāh awaiting them. Allāh explicitly states the purpose of creation, saying,

وَمَا خَلَقْتُ ٱلْجِنَّ وَٱلْإِنسَ إِلَّا لِيَعْبُدُونِ

- *I did not create jinn and humans except to worship Me.*

(Adh-Dhāriyāt, 51:56,
interpretation of the meaning)

Human beings have come to understand their purpose and how to fulfil it through the revelations received by prophets throughout history. As the Qur'ân affirms,

إِنَّآ أَوْحَيْنَآ إِلَيْكَ كَمَآ أَوْحَيْنَآ إِلَىٰ نُوحٍ وَٱلنَّبِيِّـۧنَ مِنۢ بَعْدِهِۦ

- *Verily, We have inspired you as We have inspired Noah and the Prophets after him...*

(An-Nisā', 4:163,
interpretation of the meaning)

These prophets were messengers who faithfully conveyed Allāh's message, exactly as He instructed them. This Divine guidance has been preserved in the revelations, with the Qur'ân being the final and complete revelation delivered through the last Prophet, Muḥammad ﷺ. As the Qur'ân states,

مَّا كَانَ مُحَمَّدٌ أَبَآ أَحَدٍ مِّن رِّجَالِكُمْ وَلَٰكِن رَّسُولَ ٱللَّهِ وَخَاتَمَ ٱلنَّبِيِّـۧنَ وَكَانَ ٱللَّهُ بِكُلِّ
شَىْءٍ عَلِيمًا

- *Muḥammad is not the father of any one of you men; he is Allāh's Messenger and the seal of the prophets, God knows everything.*

(Al-Aḥzāb, 33:40,
interpretation of the meaning)

Acknowledging the interconnectedness of messengers and revelations leads to the recognition that there is only one Creator, and that Muḥammad ﷺ is indeed His last messenger. Once the *Shahādah* has been embraced in its complete form, the act of worship is to live by this statement. This means, striving to fulfil the commandments of Allāh as relayed to the Messenger of Allāh.

Fundamental Spiritual Benefits

Through the *Shahādah*, a believer distances themselves from all false gods, idols, forces, and power structures that demand submission through fear or the promise of benefits. Without this detachment, a person becomes a slave to many masters such as imagined deities, power, authority, wealth, obsessive goals, and even their own desires. Allāh is critical of such people in the Qur'ân,

أَرَءَيْتَ مَنِ ٱتَّخَذَ إِلَـٰهَهُۥ هَوَىٰهُ أَفَأَنتَ تَكُونُ عَلَيْهِ وَكِيلًا

- *Have you seen the one who takes as his god his own desire? Are you to be his guardian?*

(Al-Furqān, 25:43,
interpretation of the meaning)

When a believer declares "lā ilāha" (there is no god), they are rejecting all false deities and objects of devotion, through which true freedom is attained. This detachment does not lead to rebellion but fosters indifference to all false gods, making the individual equidistant from everything that seeks to control them. It liberates the believer from the fears and pretences of life, allowing them to perceive the reality that there is only one true God. After negating all falsehoods in the mind and heart, one seeks an unshakable and trustworthy point of reference. With this realisation, they affirm "illAllāh" (except Allāh).

The phrase "illAllāh" affirms the existence of the One who sees all needs and hears all prayers, regardless of when, where, or how one prays. This realisation brings inner serenity and strength, empowering a person to face life's challenges and grow towards their true human potential. The second part of the *Shahādah*, "Muḥammadur Rasūlullāh" (Muḥammad is the Messenger of Allāh), provides a perfect human model to emulate in both daily and spiritual life. It facilitates a direct connection with Allāh through the spiritual guidance of the Prophet ﷺ.

Other Benefits

Inner Peace

By recognising that everything in the universe operates under the will of a single, all-powerful deity, believers can feel a sense of order and harmony in their lives. This understanding can mitigate feelings of chaos and uncertainty, promoting inner peace.

Believing in and practicing the *Shahādah* means having a Tawhîd-centric worldview. Ultimately, one would attain inner peace when "they give meaning to life and events in a way that satisfies the heart and mind" (Keskin, 2016, p. 24) through the lens of *Tawḥīd (*oneness of God). Nursi explains the immense benefits of believing in the One God as follows:

> Be certain of this, that the highest aim of creation and its most important result are belief in God (*iman-i billah*). And the most exalted rank

> in humanity and its highest degree are the knowledge of God (*marifatullah*) contained within belief in God. And the most radiant happiness and sweetest bounty for jinn and human beings are the love of God (*muhabbatullah*) contained within the knowledge of God. And the purest joy for the human spirit and the sheerest delight for man's heart are the rapture of the spirit (*lazzat-i ruhaniya*) contained within the love of God. Indeed, all true happiness, pure joy, sweet bounties, and untroubled pleasure lie in knowledge of God and love of God; they cannot exist without them.
>
> (Nursi, 2001, p. 265)

A natural progression to believing in Allāh should be knowledge of Allāh, which then leads to love of Allāh. In other words, joy and happiness are dependent on the believer's knowledge and love of Allāh that are founded on belief in the one God. Once these "two life-sweetening realities" have been attained, that is, knowledge and love of Allāh, a believer will be at peace in this life, no matter what comes their way. "But, he who lacks them, even if he owns the whole world, cannot find peace within himself and outside, because without faith and knowledge, he feels spiritually and physically weak, vulnerable and helpless" (Kuşpınar, 2010, p. 46). Such is the blessings that come with the belief and practice of *Shahādah*.

Being Part of a Community (Ummah)

The *Shahādah* fosters a strong sense of belonging within the Muslim community (*ummah*) (Bakar, 2012). That is, the *Shahādah* serves not only as a declaration of faith but also as a bond that unites Muslims across the world, transcending geographical, ethnic, and cultural boundaries. This sense of community is evident in various ways, such as through collective worship during daily prayers, Friday congregational prayers, and especially during the holy month of Ramaḍān. In addition to worship, the *ummah* comes together in unity during the two major Islāmic festivals, Eid al-Fitr and Eid al-Adha. These events go beyond being religious observance; they also create opportunities for social interaction, community building, and mutual support.

Research shows that being part of a religious collective contributes to positive mental health outcomes through factors such as increased social support, extended psychological resources, positive health practices, and a stronger sense of coherence (George et al., 2002). Therefore, being part of a supportive community helps alleviate feelings of loneliness and isolation. The sense of belonging and mutual support within the *ummah* offers emotional and psychological comfort, which is essential for maintaining mental well-being.

Conclusion

The five pillars of Islām serve as essential acts of worship that guide a Muslim's life spiritually, mentally, emotionally, physically, and socially. They form a comprehensive framework that fosters a deep connection with Allāh, promoting personal development, self-discipline, and emotional resilience. By engaging in these practices, Muslims are not only working towards their spiritual growth but also improving their mental well-being while contributing to a more just and cohesive society.

Each pillar facilitates detachments from worldly matters that can be obstacles to a strong connection with Allāh. Ultimately, the five pillars represent the foundation of a balanced and fulfilling life in this world, while preparing believers for the eternal rewards of the afterlife. The *Shahādah*, the first pillar of Islam, is much more than a simple declaration of faith; it is the bedrock upon which a Muslim's entire life is built. By bearing witness to the oneness of Allāh and the prophethood of Muḥammad ﷺ, believers not only affirm their place within the fold of Islam but also embark on a lifelong journey of spiritual growth. This testimony aligns one's heart, mind, and actions towards the Creator, fostering a deep sense of inner peace and purpose. The *Shahādah* serves as a constant reminder of life's ultimate truth and guides believers in all aspects of their existence, from personal worship to social interaction within the *ummah*.

References

Abdel-Khalek, A. M., & Lester, D. (2012). Constructions of religiosity, subjective well-being, anxiety, and depression in two cultures: Kuwait and USA. *International Journal of Social Psychiatry*, *58*(2), 138–145.

Abolfathi Momtaz, Y., Hamid, T. A., Ibrahim, R., Yahaya, N., & Tyng Chai, S. (2011). Moderating effect of religiosity on the relationship between social isolation and psychological well-being. *Mental Health, Religion & Culture*, *14*(2), 141–156.

Al-Qaradawi, Y. (2007). *Approaching the sunnah: Comprehension and controversy.* International Institute of Islamic Thought (IIIT).

Bakar, O. (2012). The Qur'ânic Identity of the Muslim Ummah: Tawhidic Epistemology as its Foundation and Sustainer. *ICR Journal*, *3*(3), 438–454.

Bukhârî. In book reference: Book 2, Hadith 1. English translation: Vol. 1, Book 2, Hadith 8. https://sunnah.com/bukhari:8.

George, L. K., Ellison, C. G., & Larson, D. B. (2002). Explaining the relationships between religious involvement and health. *Psychological Inquiry*, *13*, 190–200.

Husain, S. A. (1998). Religion and mental health from the Muslim perspective. In H. G. Koenig (Ed.), *Handbook of religion and mental health* (pp. 279–290). Academic Press.

Keskin, Z. (2016). Inner peace in Islam. *Australian Journal of Islamic Studies*, *1*(1), 23–38.

Keskin, Z., & Ozalp, M. (2020). An Islamic approach to environmental protection and ecologically sustainable peace in the age of the Anthropocene. In J. Camilleri &

D. Guess (Eds.), *Towards a just and ecologically sustainable peace: Navigating the great transition* (pp. 119–134). Palgrave MacMillan.

Kuşpınar, B. (2010). Justice and balance in creation. In I. M. Abu-Rabi' (Ed.), *Justice and theodicy in modern Islamic thought* (pp. 227–240). Ashgate.

Murata, S., & Chittick, W. C. (2015). *The vision of Islam*. Paragon House.

Najam, K. S., Khan, R. S., Waheed, A., & Hassan, R. (2019). Impact of Islamic practices on the mental health of Muslims. *International Dental & Medical Journal of Advanced Research*, *5*(1), 1–6.

Nursi, S. (2001). *The letters* (Ş. Vahide, Trans.). Sözler.

Turner, M. (2015). Can the effects of religion and spirituality on both physical and mental health be scientifically measured? An overview of the key sources, with particular reference to the teachings of Said Nursi. *Journal of Religion and Health*, *54*(6), 2045–2051. https://doi.org/10.1007/s10943-014-9894-3.

Yucel, S. (2024). Purpose-driven life in Islam and emotional stability: Examining said Nursi's perspective. *Australian Journal of Islamic Studies*, *9*(2), 19–36.

3 The Five Pillars

Qur'ânic Practices of *Ṣalāh* and *Zakāh*

Ṣalāh (The Five Daily Prayers)

حَـٰفِظُوا۟ عَلَى ٱلصَّلَوَٰتِ وَٱلصَّلَوٰةِ ٱلْوُسْطَىٰ وَقُومُوا۟ لِلَّهِ قَـٰنِتِينَ

- *Observe the (five obligatory) prayers, especially the middle prayer ('Asr prayer), and stand in true devotion to Allāh.*

(Al-Baqarah, Qur'ân, 2:238, interpretation of the meaning)

Ṣalāh is the praying of the five daily prayers at prescribed times. The root word ṣād lām wāw (ص ل و) occurs in 37 Chapters and appears 99 times in the Qur'ân, in three derived forms. *Ṣalāh* means to bow down, to invoke and supplicate. It has the meanings of bowing, worship, prayer, and supplication. *Ṣalāh* also means linking things together or hot connection because one connects with Allāh through the prayers. But it is no mere connection, it is such a deep and intense connection that it is referred to as a hot connection. According to the following Qur'ânic verse, everything in existence offers prayer (*ṣalāh*) to Allāh:

أَلَمْ تَرَ أَنَّ ٱللَّهَ يُسَبِّحُ لَهُۥ مَن فِى ٱلسَّمَـٰوَٰتِ وَٱلْأَرْضِ وَٱلطَّيْرُ صَـٰٓفَّـٰتٍ كُلٌّ قَدْ عَلِمَ
صَلَاتَهُۥ وَتَسْبِيحَهُۥ وَٱللَّهُ عَلِيمٌۢ بِمَا يَفْعَلُونَ

- *Do you not see that all that is in the heavens and the earth, and the birds flying in patterned ranks with wings spread out glorify Allāh. Each knows the way of its prayer (ṣalāh) and glorification. Allāh has full knowledge of all that they do.*

(An-Nūr, 24:41, interpretation of the meaning)

This verse indicates that all creatures are engaged in the glorification and worship of Allāh, though the manner of worship varies among them. Angels worship in one way, humans in another, while trees, vegetation, rocks, and minerals

DOI: 10.4324/9781003494614-3

each have their own unique forms of worship. Despite these differences, all of creation prays to Allāh in some form, illustrating that worship is a natural outcome of existence. Human beings, too, are part of this universal act of worship, but they differ in that they possess conscience and willpower, allowing them to make a conscious choice to worship Allāh. *Ṣalāh* is so important that in the following Qur'ânic verse, *Ṣalāh* is mentioned in addition to worship, even though *Ṣalāh* is a type of worship:

إِنَّنِىٓ أَنَا ٱللَّهُ لَآ إِلَـٰهَ إِلَّآ أَنَا۠ فَٱعْبُدْنِى وَأَقِمِ ٱلصَّلَوٰةَ لِذِكْرِىٓ

- *Indeed, I am Allāh. There is no deity except Me, so worship Me and establish Ṣalāh for My remembrance.*

(Ṭā-Hā, 20:14,
interpretation of the meaning)

This additional mention stresses the special merit of *Ṣalāh* relative to the other forms of worship. It is *the* pillar of faith. When worship is thought about, *Ṣalāh* would be one of the foremost types of worship that would come to mind. Such is the place of *Ṣalāh* in Islām.

The Qur'ân speaks highly of people who perform their *Ṣalāh* and promises a special place for them in the afterlife.

وَٱلَّذِينَ هُمْ عَلَىٰ صَلَوَٰتِهِمْ يُحَافِظُونَ
أُو۟لَـٰٓئِكَ هُمُ ٱلْوَٰرِثُونَ
ٱلَّذِينَ يَرِثُونَ ٱلْفِرْدَوْسَ هُمْ فِيهَا خَـٰلِدُونَ

- *They are ever mindful guardians of their Ṣalāh. Those are the inheritors, who will inherit the highest floor of Paradise (Firdaws). Therein they will abide forever.*

(Al-Mu'minūn, 23:9–11,
interpretation of the meaning)

While *Ṣalāh* benefits the practitioner in this life, this particular verse focuses on the great benefits of *Ṣalāh* for the hereafter. The use of the word "inherit" when mentioning the inheriting of the highest level of paradise, is worth noting. Inheritance is an entitlement that cannot be taken away, such as when one inherits from their parents, it is a legal right to receive what is passed down from one's parents. Similarly, a person is entitled to the highest level of paradise for being a mindful guardian of *Ṣalāh*, according to Allāh's revelation. There are many more Qur'ânic verses and *ḥadīth* that highlight the importance of *Ṣalāh* in the life of a Muslim. *Ṣalāh* is such a profound act of worship that it cannot be replaced by any other practice. Regardless of one's health condition, the obligation to perform *Ṣalāh* remains. If a person cannot stand, they may pray while sitting. If sitting is not possible, then *Ṣalāh* can be performed while lying down. In one way or another, the five daily prayers are completed without exception.

Ṣalāh as an Act of Worship

Being aware of one's limitations, weakness, and poverty, a Muslim prostrates in love and wonderment before the perfection of Allāh's Lordship, Majesty, and Compassion. Recognising the vast disparity between their finite existence and the infinite nature of Allāh, the devout Muslim humbly submits and worships. This acknowledgment of one's own inadequacy and the recognition of Allāh's supreme attributes fosters a sense of devotion and reverence. A Muslim understands that they are not self-sufficient, but rather, they are a servant dependent on Allāh's power, mercy, perfection, guidance, and much more.

This servitude is not seen as a burden but as a path to fulfillment and closeness to the Creator. The essence of worship, or *'ibādah*, in Islām is to glorify, exalt, and praise Allāh with the heart, mind, tongue, and ultimately, the whole body. While such devotion encompasses every aspect of a Muslim's life, transforming mundane actions into acts of devotion when performed with the right intention, *Ṣalāh* is the epitome of worship. It is a comprehensive act of worship that portrays great meaning through the belief embedded within the heart, the words uttered with the tongue, and reflection with the mind, all the while incorporating the necessary movements as an expression of that belief. Thus, the whole body is immersed in worship with *Ṣalāh*. When the person is standing upright and makes the intention of praying to Allāh alone, they begin by saying *Allāhu Akbar,* Allāh is the Greatest, whilst at the same time lifting both hands up to shoulder height, meaning that the world and worldly affairs are thrown behind and the worshipper is alone in the court of Allāh.

Then the worshipper bows, lowering their self in the court of Allāh and by doing so, glorifying Allāh. They also chant three times *Subḥāna Rabbīya'l-'Aẓīm*, "Glory to my Lord the Great," and by doing so, uttering in words, what their body is stating through its actions.

When the worshipper finally prostrates, they lower themselves, and their *nafs*, to the lowest point in the court of Allāh, displaying the ultimate level of physical glorification of Allāh while repeating three times *Subḥāna Rabbiya'l-A'lā*, "Glory and praise be to my Lord the Highest." The greatness of Allāh is acknowledged when the worshipper is at their physical lowest. While uttering these expressions and going through the movements that magnify the words, the worshipper meditates in their mind and heart on the greatness, perfection, and compassion of Allāh. In this way, their whole being is engaged in the act of worship, making *Ṣalāh* a complete experience.

The physical movements during *Ṣalāh* also display progressively increasing levels of submission to Allāh. In the standing-up position, with the hands together in front, the worshipper is as if saying "my hands are tied, I am ready to submit to You my Lord." Bowing is a higher level of submission than standing. Breaking the defence mechanisms of the *nafs*, it is as if the worshipper is saying "I bow down only to you, I cannot see what's in front of me. Oh Allāh, I have submitted myself to You." And then, prostration is the ultimate level of submission. It is as if the worshipper is saying,

> Oh Allāh, I am lowering my head to the same level as my feet. With respect to You, I have made myself nothing. I am completely defenseless against Your Will. Even my self does not stand between You and me. I have willingly submitted my whole self to You.

Such are the powerful movements of *Ṣalāh*.

Thus, the essence of *Ṣalāh* is to glorify, exalt, and praise Allāh as emulated in the Qur'ân:

فَسَبِّحْ بِحَمْدِ رَبِّكَ وَكُن مِّنَ ٱلسَّٰجِدِينَ

- *But celebrate the praises of your Lord and be of those who prostrate themselves in adoration.*

(Al-Ḥijr, 15:98, interpretation of the meaning)

The devotion, adoration, and exaltation expressed through *Ṣalāh* are transformative as *Ṣalāh* is performed five times a day. This devotional practice is spread throughout the day from before sunrise to after sunset, which ensures the believer is regularly reminded of their role as a servant while acknowledging the Lordship of their Creator.

Fundamental Spiritual Benefit

Ṣalāh detaches a worshipper from the daily affairs that could otherwise make the believer forget Allāh. Life is of such a nature that one can easily get drawn into the never-ending demands, or even distractions, of life. Work, children, wealth, the home, and so many other aspects of life scream for one's attention, every single day. While roles and responsibilities in life should not be neglected, a believer's roles and responsibilities towards Allāh should be the top priority and therefore never neglected.

If it is not the demands of life, it is the demands of the *nafs* that can occupy a person for hours on end, causing distraction from the purpose of creation. Being on social media for hours, spending excessive time shopping, investing large portions of the day binge watching series, and so on, can completely distance a believer from being conscious of why they were created in the first place. *Ṣalāh* serves as a reminder to what the true purpose of creation is, and most importantly, it enables a person to disconnect from their daily affairs for short but meaningful periods of time; five times a day. This then enables a person to have an intimate relationship with Allāh that no other single act can. The Prophet Muḥammad ﷺ said, "The closest that a servant is to his Lord is when he is in prostration" (Muslim (a)). In other words, the prostration, which is done during *Ṣalāh*, is when one will be the closest to Allāh. No other act can achieve such closeness according to this *ḥadīth*. Establishing prayer means that at least five times a day, Muslims are in remembrance of Allāh.

وَأَقِمِ ٱلصَّلَوٰةَ لِذِكْرِىٓ

- *And perform Ṣalāh for My remembrance.*

(Ṭā-Hā, 20:14,
interpretation of the meaning)

Humankind is forgetful by nature and easily distracted, which can lead to forgetting about Allāh, purpose of life and the Hereafter. Turning to prayer five times a day allows one to remember Allāh while also remembering one's purpose of creation. This then enables one to re-focus and re-align themselves.

Other Benefits

Detachment from the Pride of the Nafs

Ṣalāh is a detachment from the pride of the *nafs* (self). Expressing one's limits and weaknesses while recognising the greatness and glory of Allāh is the essence of *Ṣalāh*. The words uttered and the movements undertaken in *Ṣalāh* are reminders to the *nafs* that it is a servant, and that Allāh is its creator. Furthermore, *Ṣalāh* puts the *nafs* in its place by reminding it that it needs to surrender.

Alternatively, an untamed *nafs* does not want to bow down or prostrate to anyone or anything. The *nafs* likes to think it is above everything with its own power and abilities. Remember, an untamed *nafs* has pharaoh-like qualities. In the Qur'ân, when the pharaoh addresses the people, he said:

ٱلْمَلَأُ مَا عَلِمْتُ لَكُم مِّنْ إِلَـٰهٍ غَيْرِى

- *I know of no other god for you but myself.*

(Al-Qaṣaṣ, 28:38,
interpretation of the meaning)

While not all untamed *nafs'* may go to the level of declaring to be god, the *nafs* can certainly have qualities of the pharaoh whereby it likes to rely purely on itself and not recognise its need for Allāh. Thus, *Ṣalāh* is a humbling act that reminds the worshipper of their servanthood while also reminding them that they need their Creator. In this way, *Ṣalāh* is an incredible act of worship that facilitates the purification of the *nafs*, which then becomes an opportunity to connect with Allāh.

Develop Moral Behaviour

Ṣalāh is also a means to develop moral behaviour. There is a direct relationship between *Ṣalāh* and one's morality, according to the Qur'ân. Just as *Ṣalāh* should lead to good character, similarly the level of one's character becomes a measure of the quality of one's *Ṣalāh*. Allāh states in the Qur'ân:

ٱتْلُ مَا أُوحِىَ إِلَيْكَ مِ ن ٱلْكِتَٰبِ وَأَقِمِ ٱلصَّلَوٰ ةَ إِنَّ ٱلصَّلَوٰة تَنْهَىٰ عَنِ ٱلْفَحْشَآءِ
وَ ٱلْمُنكَرِ وَلَذِكْرُ ٱ لِلِ أَكْبَرُ وَ ٱ لِلُ يَعْلَ م مَا تَصْنَعُونَ

- *Recite, [O Muḥammad], what has been revealed to you of the Book and establish Ṣalāh. Indeed, Ṣalāh prohibits immorality and wrongdoing, and the remembrance of Allāh is greater. And Allāh knows what you all do.*

(Al-ʿAnkabūt, 29:45,
interpretation of the meaning)

A worshipper who stands in Allāh's presence five times a day, renewing their commitment to Allāh, would surely be more conscious of what they do in the time between two prayer times. No doubt, this kind of effect on a person's behaviour requires one to be conscious, in their heart, of the damage sins can have on them. They also must have a relationship with Allāh where they feel accountable to Allāh. When they do feel a level of accountability and they are confronted with an opportunity to do wrong or when they have an immoral inclination, especially if the time to the next *Ṣalāh* is close, there is greater reluctance to commit that immoral act. The worshipper would think, "If I commit this sin, how will I then face my Lord at my next *Ṣalāh*?" In this way, a Muslim is conscientiously prevented from doing wrong and stays on the straight path (*ṣirāṭ al-mustaqīm*). The deeper the relationship with Allāh, the more profound is the positive effects of *Ṣalāh* on one's behaviour. The five daily prayers act as a constant reminder.

Looking at this point from the opposite angle, one could measure the degree of intimacy of a Muslim's relationship with Allāh and their sincerity in *Ṣalāh*, by evaluating their character and morality. A Muslim who has good character and moral behaviour is most likely doing their prayers with high quality. That is, signs of elevated morality in a Muslim are indicative of the quality of that person's *Ṣalāh*. Similarly, if a person is visibly displaying immoral behaviour, the spiritual connection during *Ṣalāh* cannot be very strong.

Social Cohesion

From a social perspective, when *Ṣalāh* is performed with a group of people, it builds social cohesion and solidarity. *Ṣalāh* in congregation ensures that worshippers are tightly lining up in straight lines, row after row, whereby there are no distinguishments between the worshippers when making up the rows.

Great reward is promised for congregational prayer by Prophet Muḥammad ﷺ, "The reward of the congregational prayer is twenty-seven times greater (than that of the prayer offered by a person alone)" (Bukhârî (a)). This *ḥadīth* creates an incentive for Muslims to pray in congregation rather than praying alone, an incentive that has created a good habit in many Muslims to pray with others whenever possible, especially in the mosque.

There are also clear instructions on how individuals should be positioned in congregational prayer. According to a *ḥadīth*, it is important for Muslims to be standing closely together when praying. "Establish your lines [straight], for indeed the angels [pray] in lines. Align your shoulders, close the gaps, yield your hands to your brothers, and do not leave any gaps for Satan" (Abī Dāwūd). What the Prophet ﷺ was referring to here when he said, "do not leave any gaps for Satan," is the "satan" of superiority complex based on race, colour, wealth, status, and so on. Thus, in congregational prayer, a worshipper is rubbing shoulders with anyone and everyone, where superficial societal constructs are being broken, even if temporarily. There is a powerful message of brotherhood and sisterhood here, which would and should spill over into everyday practices in the wider society.

Mental Health Benefits

Ṣalāh offers significant mental benefits, contributing to both emotional well-being and cognitive health. The structured, rhythmic nature of *Ṣalāh* encourages mindfulness and a meditative state, helping to calm the mind and reduce anxiety (Ijaz et al., 2017). Engaging in regular prayer promotes relaxation by activating the parasympathetic nervous system, which is responsible for rest and recovery, reducing stress levels and promoting a sense of peace (Doufesh et al., 2014).

In addition to reducing stress, *Ṣalāh* improves focus and concentration. The act of focusing on the movements, recitations, and connection with Allāh helps train the mind to stay present and attentive, sharpening mental clarity. Furthermore, the regular practice of *Ṣalāh* can improve memory and cognitive function, as it involves learning and recalling verses from the Qur'ân and performing movements in a precise, repetitive manner.

Ultimately, "individuals who offer prayer regularly and with mindfulness have better mental health as compared with those who don't offer it regularly and with mindfulness" (Ijaz et al., 2017, p. 2297). Overall *Ṣalāh* fosters a sense of inner peace, emotional balance, and enhanced mental resilience, making it a powerful tool for mental well-being.

Physical Health Benefits

Studies on the physical aspects of *Ṣalāh* have shown that it benefits the entire body, including the heart, spine, muscles, and overall cognitive function (Reza et al., 2002). *Ṣalāh* has a positive impact on cardiovascular health by helping to lower heart rate and blood pressure, which can reduce the risk of heart disease. The rhythmic, meditative nature of *Ṣalāh*, combined with its gentle movements, promotes relaxation and lowers stress, further enhancing heart health (Chamsi-Pasha & Chamsi-Pasha, 2021).

Ṣalāh also plays a crucial role in musculoskeletal health. The various postures, such as standing, bowing, and prostrating, engage multiple muscle groups, improving muscle tone and circulation. These movements enhance flexibility, joint mobility, and postural alignment, which may reduce the risk of musculoskeletal issues, including osteoarthritis (Al-Barzinjy et al., 2009). The repetitive but controlled motions during *Ṣalāh* provide regular, moderate exercise that strengthens muscles without causing fatigue. In essence, *Ṣalāh* offers a balance of spiritual and physical activity, activating nearly all muscles of the body in a way that supports overall health.

Zakāh (Purifying Alms)

وَرَحْمَتِى وَسِعَتْ كُلَّ شَىْ ء فَسَأَكْتُبُهَا لِلَّذِي ن يَتَّقُونَ وَيُؤْتُونَ ٱلزَّكَوٰة وَ ٱلَّذِينَ
هُم بِـَٔايَـٰتِنَا يُؤْمِنُو ن

- *My Mercy extends to all things. That (Mercy) I shall ordain for those who have God-consciousness and give their Zakāh and those who believe in Our Signs.*

(Al-Aʿrāf, 7:156,
interpretation of the meaning)

Zakāh stems from the triliteral root zāy kāf wāw (و ك ز). This root word occurs in 29 Chapters and appears 59 times in the Qur'ân, in five derived forms. The word means to grow, to flourish, but it also means to purify or to be purified. These two meanings of *Zakāh* are interconnected; cleansing and purifying wealth from its impurities enables wealth to be nurtured so that it flourishes.

In Islāmic terminology, *Zakāh* is spending what has been bestowed by Allāh, in the amount and places designated by Him, for the sole purpose of physical and spiritual purification. Possessions are purified by setting aside a proportion for those in need, and, like the pruning of plants, this cutting back balances and encourages new growth.

Interestingly, *Zakāh* accompanies the mention of *Ṣalāh* in 28 verses of the Qur'ân. Here are three such examples:

وَأَقِيمُوا ٱلصَّلَوٰةَ وَءَاتُوا ٱلزَّكَوٰةَ

- *And be steadfast in prayer (Ṣalāh); practise regular charity (Zakāh)...*
  (Al-Baqarah, 2:43,
  interpretation of the meaning)

وَأَقِمْنَ ٱلصَّلَوٰةَ وَءَاتِينَ ٱلزَّكَوٰةَ

- *... and establish regular prayer (Ṣalāh) and give regular charity (Zakāh)...*
  (Al-Aḥzāb, 33:33,
  interpretation of the meaning)

وَأَقِيمُوا ٱلصَّلَوٰةَ وَءَاتُوا ٱلزَّكَوٰةَ

- *... and establish regular prayer (Ṣalāh) and give regular charity (Zakāh)...*
  (Al-Muzzammil, 73:20,
  interpretation of the meaning)

In the Qur'ân, *Zakāh* is incessantly mentioned alongside with *Ṣalāh*, as an explicit reference to the miraculous spiritual ascension achieved by humankind through prayer, which is further completed with a marvellous blessing that springs forth from almsgiving. In this way, the material is granted eternity in a world of mortality, an aspect highlighted in the Qur'ân:

وَأَقِيمُوا ٱلصَّلَوٰةَ وَءَاتُوا ٱلزَّكَوٰةَ ۚ وَمَا تُقَدِّمُوا لِأَنفُسِكُم مِّنْ خَيْرٍ تَجِدُوهُ عِندَ ٱللَّهِ

- *And establish prayer (Ṣalāh) and give Zakāh, and whatever good you put forward for yourselves, you will find it with Allāh.*
  (Al-Baqarah, 2:110, interpretation of the meaning)

The notion that *Zakāh* purifies wealth is taken very seriously, and it is believed that if *Zakāh* is not separated from wealth, it corrupts the wealth. The Prophet ﷺ said, "*Zakāh* never remains intermingled with any amount of wealth (upon which it is due) without destroying and rotting it" (Bayhaqi as cited in Qaradawi, 1973, p. 19). This is why the analogy of weeding the garden is so powerful. If the garden is not weeded, the weeds will eventually take over the beautiful flowers growing in the garden and eventually destroy the flowers.

While giving *Zakāh* may feel like a depletion in wealth, there is a very strong message in the Qur'ân and *ḥadīth* that it has the opposite effect; not only does it maintain the health of the wealth but it also helps it to grow.

Worship Aspect of Zakāh

Zakāh's significance for worship rests on the nature of poverty and richness. Allāh Almighty is the only true provider and sustainer of life, yet Allāh does not directly hand out sustenance into the hands of creatures. The Divine will is to foster movement and activity within the creation through the search for sustenance. The driving motive behind all animal and human activity is the need to earn one's living (*rizq*).

Importantly, the pursuit of sustenance acts as a means to uncover one's true purpose in life. It is through this movement that the wonders of Allāh's artistic creation are revealed and appreciated by His creatures. Consider this: if no one had to strive for their sustenance, there would be little movement or progress among humankind. The effort to earn a living, whether through farming or salaried work, drives human activity and facilitates the momentum necessary for growth, discovery, and the fulfilment of Divine purpose.

Allāh has designed human beings with Wisdom, so they depend on one another, fostering progress and development. Human civilisations are built on this interdependence, as people rely on each other to meet essential needs like food, shelter, and security. This reliance necessitates cooperation and collaboration, driving the growth and advancement of societies.

One consequence of this scheme is that the acquisition of wealth is gathered disproportionately by individuals; some have much more than what they need while others have far less than they need to survive comfortably.

However, Allāh provides enough sustenance on earth to meet the needs of all creatures. Basic living standards such as adequate food, clothing, and shelter are fundamental human rights. It is the collective responsibility of those who can to ensure that everyone has access to these essentials. Therefore, the rightful share of the poor must be returned to them from the excess wealth of the more fortunate.

By accepting the command of Allāh in the Qur'ân to pay *Zakāh*, a Muslim acknowledges that Allāh is the true owner of all wealth. A Muslim also recognises that there is enough sustenance on earth to meet the needs of all living beings and views *Zakāh* as a means to distribute that sustenance more evenly. Through this process, a Muslim purifies their assets by returning the portion that belongs to others. It also serves as a test for both the rich and the poor: will the rich show compassion and help the less fortunate, and will the poor be thankful and patient regardless of their circumstances.

Fundamental Spiritual Benefit

Zakāh detaches the worshipper from the pangs of absolute attachment and ownership of wealth, leading to a more spiritually healthy state. This leads to relative attachment, where wealth is also viewed as a trust from Allāh. The human *nafs* inherently desires to own and control unlimited amounts of wealth. Prophet Muḥammad ﷺ provides a powerful scenario to highlight this nature of a person: "If the son of Adam had a valley of gold, then he would still like to have a second. And nothing fills his mouth but dust, Allah turns to whoever repents" (Tirmidhī (a)). Thus, there is an aspect of humankind that seeks more and more wealth. Allāh states in the Qur'ân that this intense focus of accumulating wealth is a distraction from one's true purpose. By paying *Zakāh*, a Muslim breaks this insatiable appetite for wealth:

أَلْهَىٰكُمُ ٱلتَّكَاثُرُ
حَتَّىٰ زُرْتُمُ ٱلْمَقَابِرَ

- *The mutual rivalry (for piling up of worldly things) diverts you, until you go into your graves.*

(At-Takāthur, 102:1–2,
interpretation of the meaning)

Detachment from wealth can only occur if one believes that what they hold in their possession is in reality owned by Allāh and gives a portion of that to other less fortunate people. By observing the command of Allāh to pay *Zakāh,* a believer acknowledges that they are not the true owner of the wealth and that they are only a temporary holder. The result is a spiritual transformation where the worshipper learns to have a healthy level of attachment to wealth, rather than being obsessed with it. This is an important mindset which also leads to a more selfless and compassionate approach towards fellow human beings.

Other Benefits

Love of Allāh

Zakāh fosters a closer connection with Allāh by nurturing qualities that reflect His Divine names, which entail qualities that believers are encouraged to embody. These qualities, such as goodness, kindness, cleanliness, and generosity, are a mirror of Allāh's own names. Prophet Muḥammad ﷺ emphasised this point by saying:

> Indeed, Allāh is Tayyib (good), and He loves *tayyib* (what is good); He is Nazif (clean), and He loves cleanliness; He is Karim (kind), and He loves kindness; He is Jawad (generous), and He loves generosity.
>
> (Tirmidhī (b))

This hādīth beautifully illustrates the qualities that Allāh cherishes in His creation. By fulfilling the obligation of *Zakāh*, a person cultivates these very qualities within themselves. Giving to those in need nurtures a heart of generosity and compassion, mirroring Allāh's kindness and benevolence. It reminds the giver that their wealth is a trust from Allāh, meant to be shared in a way that benefits society. Thus, through *Zakāh*, a person not only aids the less fortunate but also aligns their actions with the Divine qualities Allāh loves.

A Means for Mercy

There is extra mercy promised, in the Qur'ân, for those who give *Zakāh:*

وَرَحْمَتِى وَسِعَتْ كُلَّ شَىْ ء فَسَأَكْتُبُهَا لِلَّذِي ن يَتَّقُونَ وَيُؤْتُونَ ٱلزَّكَوٰةَ وَ ٱلَّذِينَ
هُم بِآيَٰتِنَا يُؤْمِنُو ن

- *My Mercy extends to all things. That (Mercy) I shall ordain for those who have God-consciousness and give their Zakāh and those who believe in Our Signs.*

(Al-Aʿrāf, 7:156,
interpretation of the meaning)

In this Qur'ânic verse, those who pay *Zakāh* are specifically mentioned as those who will benefit from the mercy of Allāh. This highlights the important place *Zakāh* holds in drawing Allāh's mercy oneself, because giving *Zakāh* is in itself an act of mercy. This message is further emphasised by Prophet Muḥammad ﷺ, "The merciful will be shown mercy by the Most Merciful. Be merciful to those on the earth, and the One in the heavens will have mercy upon you" (Tirmidhī (c)).

The above Qur'ânic verse and *ḥadīth* denote the reciprocal nature of mercy between human beings and Allāh, the Most Merciful. It reflects the principle of reciprocity in Islām, where good deeds lead to Divine rewards. It is also an encouragement to be merciful to "those on the earth," which includes all living beings. This encompasses acts of kindness towards fellow humans, animals, and the environment. Not only does it inspire charitable actions, such as feeding the hungry, caring for orphans, and supporting those in distress, but it is also a call to action to social justice to alleviate the suffering of the oppressed and needy.

Grants Prosperity

Although giving *Zakāh* may seem to reduce one's wealth, it leads to an increase in blessings. This principle cannot be fully understood through mathematics, accounting, or by viewing it purely through the lens of cause and effect. It manifests in ways that are often unpredictable and beyond explanation.

Yet, Allāh reassures believers that by giving *Zakāh*, they will not suffer a loss, but rather they will experience gain, whether through spiritual, emotional, or even material rewards that may unfold in unexpected ways.

Allāh cautions believers about Satan's attempts to instil fear of poverty and discourage generosity. As stated in the Qur'ân:

عَلِيمٌ ٱلشَّيْطَٰنُ يَعِدُكُمُ ٱلْفَقْرَ وَيَأْمُرُكُم بِ ٱلْفَحْشَآءِ وَ ٱللَّ يَعِدُكُ م مَّغْفِرَة منْه وَفَضْلَ وَ ٱلل وَٰسِع

- *Satan threatens you with (the prospect of) poverty and bids you to the shameful deed (of stinginess), while Allāh promises you forgiveness and (great) bounties from Him. And Allāh is All-Bountiful, All-Knowing.*

(Al-Baqarah, 2:268, interpretation of the meaning)

The key is to resist Satan's trap, which makes one fear that giving *Zakāh* or *sadaqah* (charity) will lead to financial loss. Instead, believers should trust in Allāh's promise of forgiveness and abundant rewards, knowing that generosity will never lead to true impoverishment. On this point, Prophet Muḥammad ﷺ said, "*Sadaqah* never causes loss in your wealth" (Muslim (b)). In essence, *Zakāh* is a process of ensuring the continuance of wealth rather than its loss. Furthermore, being charitable earns the *du'ā'* of the angels. Prophet Muḥammad ﷺ explains,

> Two angels descend each day. One of them praying, 'Oh Allāh! Bestow prosperity on the wealth of those who are charitable,' and the other imploring, 'Oh Allāh! Destroy the wealth of the miser'.
>
> (Bukhârî (b))

It is important to note, the *du'ā'* of angels is not like the *du'ā'* of a human being. Angels are sinless pure beings who do nothing but worship Allāh. This is unlike human beings who are immersed or touched by sins in one way or another. Therefore, receiving the *du'ā'* of angels is a great blessing, which can only produce great outcomes.

While *Zakāh* grants prosperity for this life, most importantly, it also grants prosperity in the afterlife. Afterall, the earth is merely like an inn, found on a highway that takes the traveller to the pre-planned abode, the *ākhirah* (afterlife). *Zakāh* and *sadaqah* commences in this world a process of eternalising property in preparation for the hereafter as stressed by the Prophet ﷺ, "The son of Adam boasts, 'My wealth! My wealth! O son of Adam, have you truly earned any wealth but what you ate and consumed, or put on and wore out, or spent in charity so it remained?'" (Muslim (c)). This *ḥadīth* defines what true wealth is and an important part of that definition is that the wealth given as charity is the wealth that one truly possesses because it is an investment in the afterlife. The charity given does not need to be large amounts for it to be an investment, for Prophet Muḥammad ﷺ said, "Protect yourselves from hellfire, even if it be with half a date" (Bukhârî (c)).

Zakāh is such a powerful act of worship that it not only brings material blessings in this life but also immense rewards in the hereafter. By giving *Zakāh*, believers align themselves with Allāh's promises of forgiveness and bounty, overcoming the fear of poverty that Satan instils. The benefits of charity extend far beyond what can be calculated, encompassing both spiritual prosperity and protection from harm.

Social Cohesion

Zakāh plays a significant role in fostering social cohesion by bridging the economic gap between the wealthy and the poor. Through *Zakāh*, wealth is redistributed, ensuring that the basic needs of the less fortunate are met, which reduces economic inequality and promotes a sense of solidarity within the community (Wiliasih et al., 2011). Social Return on Investment which can play out as the "good done in a community from a non-profit venture" (Brooks, 2007, p. 405) is believed to have a significant positive impact on trust and social cohesion within a community. *Zakāh* can greatly contribute to this good.

Zakāh helps create a more balanced and just society, where the wealthier members of the community support those in need, reducing feelings of alienation and marginalisation (El-Ashker & Wilson, 2010). In this way, *Zakāh* serves as a mechanism for wealth distribution, promoting a more inclusive and united community.

Mental Health Benefits

A person paying *Zakāh* has a settled state of mind and conscious knowing that they have contributed positively to the lives of individuals and society as a whole. This clears the believer's mind and conscience. A Muslim would also subjectively think that since they have given the rightful portion of the poor in their excess wealth, they have purified their wealth.

Research has shown that giving in charity is an "avenue to happiness that is often overlooked: people may in fact feel a rush of happiness when they help others" (Liu & Aaker, 2008, p. 553). This notion that giving makes people "both happier and healthier" (Brooks, 2007, p. 405) is supported by various studies that highlight the psychological and physiological benefits of generosity. Acts of giving not only promote positive emotions but also reduce stress and foster a sense of purpose and connection. By contributing to the well-being of others, individuals often experience enhanced self-esteem and life satisfaction, reinforcing the idea that helping others leads to personal fulfilment. This reciprocal relationship between giving and well-being suggests that charitable acts are beneficial not only for recipients but also for the givers themselves, creating a cycle of positivity and emotional well-being.

Conclusion

Ṣalāh and *Zakāh* are not only essential pillars of Islam but are transformative practices that deeply impact both the individual and the community. Through *Ṣalāh*, believers strengthen their connection to Allāh, finding peace, humility, and discipline in their daily lives. *Zakāh*, by purifying wealth and fostering generosity, bridges social gaps, promoting justice and compassion in society. Together, these acts of worship cultivate spiritual growth, moral integrity, and social harmony. They serve as constant reminders of a Muslim's purpose, guiding believers to lead balanced lives grounded in faith.

References

Abī Dāwūd. Sunan Abī Dāwūd 666. https://www.abuaminaelias.com/dailyhadithonline/2022/08/28/salah-sufuf/.

Al-Barzinjy, N., Rasool, M. T., & Al-Dabbagh, T. Q. (2009). Islamic praying and osteoarthritis changes of weight bearing joints. *Duhok Medical*, *3*(1), 33–44.

Brooks, A. C. (2007). Does giving make us prosperous? *Journal of Economics and Finance*, *31*(3), 403–418.

Bukhârî (a). In-book reference: Book 10, Hadith 46. English translation: Vol. 1, Book 11, Hadith 621. https://sunnah.com/bukhari:649.

Bukhârî (b). In-book reference: Book 24, Hadith 45. English translation: Vol. 2, Book 24, Hadith 522. https://sunnah.com/bukhari:1442.

Bukhârî (c). In-book reference: Book 24, Hadith 21. English translation: Vol. 2, Book 24, Hadith 498. https://sunnah.com/bukhari:1417.

Chamsi-Pasha, M., & Chamsi-Pasha, H. (2021). A review of the literature on the health benefits of Salat (Islamic prayer). *Medical Journal of Malaysia*, *76*(1), 93–97.

Doufesh, H., Ibrahim, F., Ismail, N. A., & Wan Ahmad, W. A. (2014). Effect of Muslim prayer (salat) on α electroencephalography and its relationship with autonomic nervous system activity. *Journal of Alternative and Complementary Medicine*, *20*(7), 558–562.

El-Ashker, A., & Wilson, R. (2010). *Islamic economics: A short history*. Brill Academic Publishers.

Ijaz, S., Khalily, M. T., & Ahmad, I. (2017). Mindfulness in *Ṣalāh* prayer and its association with mental health. *Journal of Religion and Health*, *56*(6), 2297–2307. https://doi.org/10.1007/s10943-017-0413-1.

Liu, W., & Aaker, J. (2008). The happiness of giving: The time-ask effect. *Journal of Consumer Research*, *35*(3), 543–557.

Muslim (a). In-book reference: Book 4, Hadith 245. English translation: Book 4, Hadith 979. https://sunnah.com/muslim:482.

Muslim (b). In-book reference: Book 45, Hadith 90. English translation: Book 32, Hadith 6264. https://sunnah.com/muslim:2588.

Muslim (c). In-book reference: Book 55, Hadith 4. English translation: Book 42, Hadith 7061. https://sunnah.com/muslim:2958a.

Qaradawi, Y. (1973). *Fiqh al-zakah.* King Abdul Aziz University.

Reza, M. F., Urakami, Y., & Mano, Y. (2002). Evaluation of a new physical exercise taken from salat (prayer) as a short-duration and frequent physical activity in the rehabilitation of geriatric and disabled patients. *Annals of Saudi Medicine*, *22*(3–4), 177–180.

Tirmidhī (a). In-book reference: Book 36, Hadith 34. English translation: Vol. 4, Book 10, Hadith 2337. https://sunnah.com/tirmidhi:2337.

Tirmidhī (b). In-book reference: Book 43, Hadith 72. English translation: Vol. 5, Book 41, Hadith 2779. https://sunnah.com/tirmidhi:2799.

Tirmidhī (c). In-book reference: Book 27, Hadith 30. English translation: Vol. 4, Book 1, Hadith 1924. https://sunnah.com/tirmidhi:1924.

Wiliasih, R., Usman, H., Marzuki, K., & Mardoni, Y. (2011). Relationship between quality of life and regular zakah exercise. *International Journal of Business and Social Science, 2*(16), 173–180.

4 The Five Pillars

Qur'ânic Practices of *Ṣawm* and *Ḥajj*

Ṣawm (Fasting)

يَٰٓأَيُّهَا ٱلَّذِينَ ءَامَنُوا۟ كُتِبَ عَلَيْكُمُ ٱلصِّيَامُ كَمَا كُتِبَ عَلَى ٱلَّذِينَ مِن قَبْلِكُمْ لَعَلَّكُمْ تَتَّقُونَ

- *O believers! Fasting is prescribed for you, as it was for those before you, so perhaps you will become mindful (of Allāh).*

(Al-Baqarah, 2:183,
interpretation of the meaning)

Fasting (*Ṣawm*) stems from the triliteral root ṣād wāw mīm (ص و م). This root word occurs in six Chapters and appears 14 times in the Qur'ân, in three derived forms. *Ṣawm* is also mentioned in many *ḥadīth*. *Ṣawm* literally means to keep a distance from something or to refrain from it. In the Islāmic context, *Ṣawm* is practiced in Ramaḍān, which is the ninth month of the Islāmic calendar. Islāmic fasting is the practice of abstaining from food, drink, sexual activity, and anything which substitutes food and drink.

Fasting is an act of worship commanded by Allāh in the Qur'ân to cultivate *taqwā*, piety, or God-consciousness, a state that Allāh loves to see in a person. Fasting during Ramaḍān has many other benefits, and one of those benefits are mentioned in the following verse:

شَهْرُ رَمَضَانَ ٱلَّذِىٓ أُنزِلَ فِيهِ ٱلْقُرْءَانُ
وَلِتُكْمِلُوا۟ ٱلْعِدَّةَ وَلِتُكَبِّرُوا۟ ٱللَّهَ عَلَىٰ مَا هَدَىٰكُمْ وَلَعَلَّكُمْ تَشْكُرُونَ

- *... The month of Ramaḍān, in which the Qur'ân was sent down...so that you can complete the number of the days required, and exalt Allāh for He has guided you, and perhaps you will be grateful.*

(Al-Baqarah, 2:185,
translation of the meaning)

Fasting generates gratitude in the person fasting. To abstain from necessities, such as food and water, allows a person to realise how important those basic

DOI: 10.4324/9781003494614-4

needs are, as they feel the impacts of its absence throughout the day. Furthermore, fasting is a special type of worship that Allāh says He will reward individually:

> Every (good) deed of the son of Adam would be multiplied, a good deed receiving a tenfold to seven hundredfold rewards. Allāh, the Exalted and Majestic, has said: Except for fasting, for it is done for Me and I will give a reward for it, for one abandons his passion and food for My sake. There are two occasions of joy for one who fasts, joy when he breaks it, and joy when he meets his Lord, and the breath (of an observer of fast) is sweeter to Allah than the fragrance of musk.
>
> (Muslim (a))

So many special aspects of fasting are mentioned in this *ḥadīth*. Firstly, the reward of fasting is not known; the reward will be a special surprise for the believer in the afterlife. Just as one receives great joy from the first sip of water and the first bite of food after a whole day of fasting, there will be immense joy when one finds out the reward they will receive for their fasts, in the afterlife.

Al-Ghazzālī (1992) states that fasting is one quarter of faith. He draws this conclusion based on several *ḥadīth* which he cites together. In one *ḥadīth*, the Prophet says, "Adhere to fasting as there is nothing equal to it." In another *ḥadīth*, "Fasting comprises half of patience" and then "Patience comprises half of belief." Ghazzali states that fasting therefore equals one quarter of belief whereby its reward transcends any type of calculation (Al-Ghazzālī, 1992, p. 8). Such is the reward of fasting.

Worship Aspect of Fasting

There are two worship aspects of fasting. Firstly, fasting acknowledges the existence of thousands of blessings on this earth for the benefit of human beings while acknowledging that Allāh is the true owner and provider of all those blessings. Secondly, fasting for a Muslim is a profound act of thanksgiving, where one expresses their sincere appreciation for the sustenance received from Allāh. On this point, Nursi states, that true thanksgiving is, "to recognize that the bounties come directly from Him; it is to appreciate their worth and to perceive one's own need for them" (Nursi, 2001, p. 467).

Based on Nursi's words, there are three aspects to true thankfulness which are experienced with fasting:

1. To recognise that all sustenance comes directly from Allāh. Abstaining from food and drink during fasting, as commanded by Allāh, acknowledges that everything originates from Him. Only the One who bestows

blessings has the authority to command us to refrain from consuming them.

2 To truly appreciate the value of sustenance. Only when one experiences hunger and thirst, can they fully comprehend the worth of food and drink. Fasting enables this understanding.

3 To recognise one's need and dependence on sustenance. Only when one is deprived of food and water for extended periods of time, can one truly appreciate their reliance on the fundamental necessities of life.

Fundamental Spiritual Benefit

The fundamental spiritual benefit of fasting is to detach the worshipper from physical desires and emotional impulses. This is achieved through the effects fasting has on the *nafs*. Fasting addresses a fundamental weakness in the *nafs* which is that it acts on impulses at any opportunity, especially if it has not been tamed. An untamed *nafs* inherently thinks it is free and unrestricted. Such a *nafs* wishes for and imagines lordship and free, arbitrary action. The *nafs* assaults the world as though it possesses a body made of steel and imagines itself to be undying and eternal.

Through fasting, the rebellious tendencies of the carnal *nafs* are gradually dampened and pacified through a systematic submission of these tendencies to the Divine Will. In this way, one's absolute dependence on these desires and impulses is somewhat detached and transformed into a relative dependence. Fasting humbles the *nafs*, reminding it of its weakness and dependence on Allāh for even the most basic provisions. It reinforces the truth that Allāh is the ultimate owner of the *nafs*, stripping away any illusion it may have of self-sovereignty. This awareness elevates a believer's spiritual connection, enabling them to approach their Creator in supplication and ascend through the ranks of spiritual growth. Fasting also exercises the willpower to attain self-control that is needed for success in every facet of life. By fasting consecutively for 29–30 days, the human willpower is truly sharpened, and self-control becomes a habit. Many people find themselves instinctively maintaining restraint after Ramaḍān, as if they are still fasting. For some time, they continue to avoid impulsive overeating for extended periods. This sharpened willpower has a ripple effect, positively influencing every area of life.

One may ask how the benefits of fasting for one month of the year can be maintained throughout the year. Such maintenance is possible through the Sunnah fasts. The Prophet ﷺ encouraged Muslims to fast on the following days, as Sunnah fasts:

- Six days of Shawwal (the month after Ramaḍān)
- Muharram 10 (Ashura) and the days immediately preceding and following it.
- Most of Sha'ban (the month preceding Ramaḍān)

- Every Monday and Thursday
- 13th, 14th, and 15th days of each month, known as the white days
- He also permitted those who can fast every other day (fast of Prophet Dawud), for those who are able to commit to such a fast.

The Sunnah fasts are taken very seriously. Al Ghazzālī (1992) explains that most scholars discourage allowing more than four days to pass between fasts, as doing so can harden the heart, foster bad habits, and increase susceptibility to desires and indulgence. While it may be challenging for many Muslims to consistently observe Sunnah fasts, even fulfilling the obligatory fasts of Ramaḍān with sincerity and mindfulness can have a transformative impact.

An experiment was done in 1960s by Walter Mischel at a preschool in Stanford University where the ability of four-year-old children to resist temptations was tested. In a room, a marshmallow was placed, and the child was told that he or she can eat the marshmallow now or wait for a while and then have two marshmallows. In other words, the children would be rewarded for waiting. While some children waited, others ate the one marshmallow immediately. The same children were tracked for 14 years to see how they rated in life (Mischel, 2014).

Those who had resisted temptation at four were now more socially competent, personally effective, self-assertive, and better able to cope with the frustrations of life. Also, those who had waited patiently at four were far superior as students to those who acted on whim (Mischel, 2014). This experiment underscores the importance of having self-discipline in life, which means resisting impulses. On this point, Coleman (2006) argues that resisting impulse is arguably the most essential physiological skill. It forms the foundation of emotional self-control, as emotions naturally trigger various urges to act.

While one may think it is left to their fate whether they were the child who ate the one marshmallow or waited for a while so they can then be rewarded with another marshmallow, this is not the case. Fasting can develop this skill of self-discipline and self-control, which can lead to resisting impulsive behaviour. This can then lead to success in every facet of life, especially if the Sunnah fasts are undertaken in addition to fasting in the month of Ramaḍān.

Other Benefits

The Spirit Thrives

Spiritual and physical aspects of the human being compete with one another to exercise their dominance over the individual. If one dominates, the other subsides. When there is overconsumption of food, it is an over-indulgence that then feeds the *nafs*. This is to the detriment of the spirit. Nursi (1995) states, "It is because of this that for centuries those closest to God have accustomed themselves to discipline and to eating and drinking little in order to be perfected" (p. 472). Overeating comes at a spiritual cost and to combat this, the desires of the physical body need to be managed, even if it is for a limited period.

Thus, there is a need to shift the pointer of the scale in the favour of spirituality to find a balanced development for the individual. It becomes a reminder to the body of its true purpose of existing, which is to worship Allāh. It also reminds the believer that their ultimate purpose is not to indulge in physical desires, which include eating, drinking, and sexual activity. Hunger through fasting gives the spirit a chance to get out of the physical dominance. Furthermore, by suppressing the lower demands of *nafs*, fasting allows a person to be open to the secrets of the Qur'ân when reading it during the month of Ramaḍān. This is of great significance, particularly since the Qur'ân was revealed during the month of Ramaḍān, as mentioned in Chapter 97 of the Qur'ân. Such a state of spiritual openness allows a person to connect with the Qur'ân in the holiest month of the year.

Creates Empathy

Fasting allows the wealthy to experience the reality of hunger, offering a glimpse into what it means to lack the resources to meet basic needs. Only by enduring hunger and thirst can one truly grasp the challenges that the poor face daily. While fasting provides just a brief insight into the struggles of the less fortunate, it is often enough to awaken empathy and compassion within a person. Even as one fasts, they remain mindful of when it is time to break their fast, often counting down the minutes until sunset. In those moments, it is common to think, "At least I know when iftar is, and I know exactly when I can eat." In contrast, many poor people, who are deprived of food and water due to lack of access, have no certainty about when their next meal will come. This realisation stirs empathy in the fasting person, deepening their awareness of the struggles faced by those in need.

Additionally, a common reaction from non-Muslims when they learn about fasting is, "Really, you can't even drink water?" For many fasting Muslims, this highlights another point of empathy. While the reassurance of having clean water to drink at the end of the day brings comfort, it also serves as a sobering reminder that millions of people around the world lack access to safe drinking water. This awareness deepens the spiritual and empathetic dimensions of fasting. This kind of empathy reminds the wealthy of the hardships of hunger and thirst, often inspiring them to be more charitable towards the poor. Fasting serves this purpose by creating a bridge of understanding between the rich and the poor. It fosters a relationship of compassion and generosity, which can significantly contribute to social justice and harmony within society.

Social Cohesion

Ramaḍān is one of the most social months for Muslims, marked by gatherings of various sizes where they come together to break their fast. These gatherings range from intimate family meals at homes to larger events in mosques, reception halls, and parks. It is a common practice for Muslims to invite others to join in the celebration of iftar, fostering a sense of community and shared gratitude during this sacred time.

This beautiful cultural practice is deeply rooted in the *ḥadīth*, "Whoever gives food to a fasting person to break their fast will have a reward like that of the fasting person, without diminishing their reward in the slightest" (Ibn Mājah). In essence, for every fasting person that is fed, the host earns the same reward as the fasting person, without reducing the fasting person's reward. This means that such gatherings not only foster community but also multiply the spiritual rewards of fasting, simply by coming together and providing food for others who have fasted.

Wealthy Muslims often organise large dinners for the poor, while friends and family compete to host loved ones, enhancing social cohesion and strengthening interpersonal relationships. The empathy cultivated through fasting, combined with the promise of extra reward for good deeds during Ramaḍān, motivates many Muslims to be especially generous in their charitable donations to the poor and needy throughout this holy month. This generosity not only benefits those in need but also deepens the sense of community and compassion within society.

Social cohesion is further strengthened by the widespread practice of praying *Tarāwīḥ*, a highly recommended Sunnah. Every night during Ramaḍān, mosques are filled with worshippers who gather for *Tarāwīḥ* prayers, fostering a deep sense of community and shared devotion. This collective act of worship brings Muslims together, reinforcing bonds and creating an atmosphere of unity and spirituality within local mosques.

Mental Health Benefits

Fasting, particularly during Ramaḍān, has been shown to have a significant positive impact on mental health, including psychological and emotional well-being. Research highlights that individuals who fast during Ramaḍān experience improvements in various mental health aspects such as reduced physical symptoms, better sleep quality, decreased anxiety, improved social functioning, and lower levels of depression (Mousavi et al., 2014; Sadeghi & Mazaheri, 2005). The psychological benefits of fasting can be attributed to a combination of factors, including the sense of accomplishment that comes from practicing self-control and discipline. Abstaining from food, drink, and other temptations during daylight hours also fosters a heightened sense of self-awareness and spiritual focus, which can lead to enhanced emotional resilience and mental clarity.

Additionally, the social aspect of Ramaḍān can have a positive effect on the mental health of Muslims as they come together for *ifṭār* and attend *Tarāwīḥ* prayers at the local mosque. This communal aspect of fasting provides emotional support and strengthens social bonds, which can contribute to improved emotional well-being.

Biologically, fasting has been linked to changes in neurotransmitter activity, particularly serotonin and dopamine, which play key roles in mood regulation. Studies have found that fasting can boost serotonin levels, leading to improved mood and reduced feelings of anxiety and depression (Fond et al., 2013). Overall, fasting not only contributes to physical health but also supports mental and emotional well-being, fostering a holistic sense of balance.

Physical Health Benefits

The physical benefits of fasting have become a huge focus in the last 10–20 years as the benefits of fasting have emerged through research. Fasting, particularly as practiced in Ramaḍān, provides numerous physical health benefits. Research suggests that fasting can lead to improved metabolic health by reducing blood sugar levels, enhancing insulin sensitivity and promoting weight loss, which lowers the risk of type 2 diabetes (Norouzy et al., 2013).

Fasting also supports cardiovascular health by lowering blood pressure, cholesterol levels, and inflammation, which are key factors in heart disease prevention (Kul et al., 2014). Additionally, fasting encourages the body to detoxify by breaking down fat stores, allowing for the release of toxins stored in fat tissue. The process of autophagy, a cellular cleansing mechanism, is also enhanced during fasting, helping the body remove damaged cells and regenerate healthier ones (Longo & Mattson, 2014). These combined benefits make fasting a powerful tool for improving overall physical health.

Ḥajj

وَلِلَّهِ عَلَى ٱلنَّاسِ حِجُّ ٱلْبَيْتِ مَنِ ٱسْتَطَاعَ إِلَيْهِ سَبِيلًا

- *Pilgrimage to the House is a duty owed to Allāh by all who can afford a way to it.*

(Āl ʿImrān, 3:97,
interpretation of the meaning)

Ḥajj stems from the triliteral root ḥā jīm jīm (ح ج ج). This root word occurs in ten Chapters and appears 33 times in the Qur'ân, in five derived forms. Twelve of these mentions are in relation to *Ḥajj*, a pilgrimage to the sacred lands as a pillar of Islām. The Arabic word *Ḥajj* literally means to continuously strive to reach one's goal. In Islāmic terminology, *Ḥajj* refers to once in a lifetime journey (pilgrimage) with the intention of visiting holy places and performing certain religious rites in accordance with the way prescribed by Prophet Muḥammad ﷺ.

Ḥajj consists of visiting a number of sacred places such as Ka'bah, Mt. Arafa, and performing specific rites from the 8th to 13th Dhū'l-Ḥijjah, the 12th month of the Islāmic calendar. *Ḥajj* is one of the five pillars of Islām that must be performed once in lifetime for those who have the wealth and the health to be able to complete it.

Ḥajj has a number of important rituals associated with it, including:

- Putting on *iḥrām,* the two pieced cloth.
- Tawaf (circumambulating) the Ka'bah seven times.
- A fast walk between *Ṣafā* and *Marwah* near Ka'bah.
- Visiting and staying at *Mina*, *'Arafa*, and *Muzdalifa.*
- Throwing pebbles at three fixed places in *Mina.*
- Shaving or trimming hair.
- Sacrificing of an animal, which is distributed to the poor.

The following verse states that *Ḥajj* is compulsory:

فِيهِ ءَايَٰتٌ بَيِّنَٰتٌ مَّقَامُ إِبْرَٰهِيمَ وَمَن دَخَلَهُۥ كَانَ ءَامِنًا وَلِلَّهِ عَلَى ٱلنَّاسِ حِجُّ
ٱلْبَيْتِ مَنِ ٱسْتَطَاعَ إِلَيْهِ سَبِيلًا وَمَن كَفَرَ فَإِنَّ ٱللَّهَ غَنِىٌّ عَنِ ٱلْعَٰلَمِينَ

- *In it, there are clear signs, and the Station of Abraham. Whoever enters it is in security. Pilgrimage to the House is a duty owed to Allāh by all who can afford a way to it. And whoever refuses, or is ungrateful to Allāh, Allāh is absolutely independent of all creatures.*

(Āl ʿImrān, 3:97,
interpretation of the meaning)

There is also the following Qur'ânic verse which notes the necessity for all Muslims, no matter where they live, to complete their duty of *Ḥajj*:

وَأَذِّن فِى ٱلنَّاسِ بِٱلْحَجِّ يَأْتُوكَ رِجَالًا وَعَلَىٰ كُلِّ ضَامِرٍ يَأْتِينَ مِن كُلِّ فَجٍّ عَمِيقٍ

- *Publicly proclaim the (duty of) Pilgrimage for all humankind, that they come to you on foot and on lean camels, coming from every faraway point.*

(Al-Ḥajj, 22:27,
interpretation of the meaning)

Ḥajj is an incredible journey that includes exaltation, glorification, and praising of Allāh through the various rituals undertaken. Muslims exalt Allāh by showing up in mass, as though saying "You are greater than myself and above the whole of humanity. Here we are ready to worship you in mass." Pilgrims glorify Allāh by going around the Ka'bah, as though saying, "Just as we are circling the one and only Ka'bah, the oldest place of worship on earth, we only obey you the Absolute One worthy of worship." Pilgrims praise Allāh through the collective *duʿā'* and remembrance of Allāh in the plains of Mt. Arafa, as well as in other holy places.

Worship Aspect of Ḥajj

Ḥajj is more than connecting with the historical legacy of Islām. It is a form of collective worship. It is a way of establishing a connection with monotheism and its human legacy symbolised by Prophet Abraham (pbuh) as well as the first human and first prophet, Adam (pbuh), respectively. As pointed out in the verse, all creatures glorify, praise, and worship Allāh in the language of their natural disposition, and they have done so throughout history:

سَبَّحَ لِلَّهِ مَا فِى ٱلسَّمَـٰوَٰتِ وَٱلْأَرْضِ ۖ وَهُوَ ٱلْعَزِيزُ ٱلْحَكِيمُ

- *Whatever is in the heavens and the earth glorifies Allāh; and He is the All-Glorious with irresistible might, the All-Wise.*

(Al-Ḥadīd, 57:1, interpretation of the meaning)

Such worship occurs individually when creatures display the wonders of Allāh's creativity and live in accordance with the purposes of their creation. It also occurs when creatures worship collectively by obeying the call of Allāh in large numbers. All great mass animal migrations and synchronised blossoming of all plants in springtime are examples of collective acts of worship seen in the natural world. Believers also obey the call of Allāh by turning up in their millions at the time of *Ḥajj*. The central aims of worship; exalting, glorifying, and praising Allāh occur individually and collectively, facilitating an incredible alignment with one's *fiṭrah* and the creation around them.

Another universal act of worship that can be observed is the way all things orbit a central point. Electrons orbit the nucleus in an atom, the Earth and planets orbit the sun, and the entire solar system orbits the centre of the Milky Way. In a profound reflection of this cosmic rhythm, Muslims participate in this mode of worship by circumambulating the Ka'bah during *Ḥajj*. This act symbolises a deep synchronisation with the universe and all of creation, as the pilgrims circle the Ka'bah, the first house built for the worship of the one true God. The continuous turning around the Ka'bah serves as a powerful representation of monotheism, where Allāh is the eternal centre of life and existence. This motion, echoing the natural order of the cosmos, is an affirmation that all creation revolves around the singular Creator, symbolising unity, harmony, and submission to the Divine Will.

Furthermore, Mt. Arafa has a significant place in the history of humanity. It is the place where the first man, Adam (pbuh) and his partner Eve sincerely repented and received forgiveness for their mistake committed in Paradise. Similarly, Muslims turn up in millions at the same place to repent for their sins and ask for forgiveness.

As people from all races and nations gather at the spiritual epicentre of the world, the Ka'bah, they are affirming their common ancestry with Adam (pbuh) and their spiritual ancestry with Abraham (pbuh) while realigning themselves with monotheism in unison with their Muslim brothers and sisters who have gathered at this spiritual centre from all around the world.

Fundamental Spiritual Benefit

The two fundamental spiritual benefits of *Ḥajj* are the forgiveness of all sins and overcoming racism. If one does not clear the sins of the past, it leads one to despair of getting close to Allāh. And if racism is not removed from the heart and mind, it will consume the spiritual heart causing many spiritual diseases such as arrogance, pride, and injustice, which can destroy the spiritual heart.

Regarding the first fundamental spiritual benefit, if sins continue to burden a person, they can lead to despair, gradually eroding motivation and enthusiasm for worship. This, in turn, may weaken one's spiritual connection with Allāh. The shame and fear of facing Allāh with a heavy burden of sins can cause a person to distance themselves from Him. To prevent sins from becoming an obstacle between the self and Allāh, they must be cleansed. This purification begins by settling any human rights before the pilgrimage and continues with sincere repentance, especially during *Ḥajj*, with the pinnacle of forgiveness sought at Arafah.

The following *ḥadīth* states how a person will be pure like a newborn after doing *Ḥajj*: "Whoever performs *Ḥajj* to this house, Ka'bah, and does not commit any obscenity and wrongdoing, he, or she, will come out as the day he, or she, was born – pure and free from sins" (Bukhârî). This promise from Allāh, based on the words of Prophet Muḥammad ﷺ, gives hope and optimism to anyone who is a sinner, which is everyone.

The impact of *Ḥajj* on one's understanding of their sins goes even deeper. *Ḥajj* serves as a transformative template that can be applied repeatedly throughout life. After experiencing the act of repentance during *Ḥajj*, a person gains the awareness that, whenever they commit sins, they can always turn back to Allāh in sincere repentance and seek His forgiveness, just as they did during *Ḥajj*. This experience instils a lifelong habit of returning to Allāh for mercy and renewal.

The second fundamental spiritual benefit addresses the issue of racism that would otherwise prevent spiritual development. This is because racism leads to a superiority complex over other races or it justifies transgression of the rights of other people. There needs to be a display of equality at such a magnitude that it would make one realise that feelings of race superiority are harmful. *Ḥajj* enables a Muslim to realise the universality of Islām as they see Muslims from all over the world, from all nationalities and races. All these people, despite their different races, come together for exactly the same reason; to gain the pleasure of Allāh through the completion of certain rituals, purely for the sake of Allāh. Muslims realise the universality of Islām, noting that it is not exclusive to one race or one colour.

A pilgrim develops an acute sense of equality of human beings in practice rather than just theory. It simulates the Day of Judgment when masses gather in one place wearing only a two-pieced white garment without any stiches. In addition, this uniform dressing is an expression of the absolute equality of human beings where culture and status become oblivious.

It was this experience that led to the transformation of Malcolm X as he explains,

> There were tens of thousands of pilgrims, from all over the world. They were of all colours, from blue-eyed blondes to black-skinned Africans. But we were all participating in the same ritual, displaying a spirit of unity and brotherhood that my experiences in America had led me to believe never could exist...

Other Benefits of Ḥajj

Remembrance of the Day of Judgement

During *Ḥajj*, masses are moving in unison and with a common dress, stripped of all worldly possessions, enacting the Day of Judgement. It is a gathering where the rich cannot be distinguished from the poor, the educated from the uneducated, the elite from the common. At *Ḥajj*, all the identities one carries in their everyday life strips away. This can make the pilgrim feel bare and vulnerable, which has powerful spiritual benefits as it helps the pilgrim to understand the importance of the Qur'ânic verse:

يَوْمَ لَا يَنفَعُ مَالٌ وَلَا بَنُونَ
إِلَّا مَنْ أَتَى ٱللَّهَ بِقَلْبٍ سَلِيمٍ

- *The Day when neither wealth nor children will be of any benefit, but only those who come before Allāh with a pure heart.*

(Ash-Shuʿarāʾ, 26:88–89,
interpretation of the meaning)

One thing that does not get stripped away at *Ḥajj* is the spiritual heart. If anything, it comes alive even more. Thus, during *Ḥajj*, when one leaves behind their family, home, and profession, it gives the pilgrim the opportunity to focus on their heart, and as highlighted in the above Qur'ânic verse, it is the heart that will matter on the Day of Judgement.

Wearing of the *iḥrām* plays an important role in being reminded of the Day of Judgement. Being wrapped in while cloths is a good reminder of the white shrouds that everyone will be wrapped in when they die. This is particularly amplified in two places, Arafah and Muzdalifa.

On the day Arafah, millions of Muslims are seen on the planes of Arafah, pleading with their Lord to forgive them. While there are massive crowds, everyone is alone in their own world, thinking about their life and their deeds, connecting with Allāh at a personal level. The intense heat of the sun is felt as there is not a single tree to seek shade under. In relation to the Day of Judgement, Prophet Muḥammad ﷺ said, "On the Day of Resurrection, the sun would draw so close to the people that there would be left only a distance of one mile" (Muslim (b)). Thus, the similarity between Arafah and the Day of Judgement is striking.

Muzdalifah is another experience where the Day of Judgement is greatly exemplified. As thousands sleep under the stars, there is this immense feeling of it being like a grave, as people sleep in their simple white cloths, again, looking like the shrouds they will be wrapped in when they die. The ocean of pilgrims sleeping in their *iḥrāms* is a true reminder of a grave. The main difference is, the people sleeping in Muzdalifah are on top of the soil, while in the grave, they will be under the soil. Then, at *Fajr* time, as everyone wakes up, it is as though they are all being resurrected, as they will be on the Day of Judgement. Such is the power of *Ḥajj* in remembering the Day of Judgement.

Developing Mental and Physical Strength

Ḥajj exercises and develops numerous mental skills such as determination, perseverance, patience, and self-control in challenging conditions. It is truly a physically demanding pillar of Islām, and arguably the most physical of all, as it requires extensive walking, often under harsh weather conditions. Given that Saudi Arabia is a desert, pilgrims frequently find themselves enduring intense heat, especially during rituals that must be performed at specific times. For instance, the journey from Mina to the Jamārāt often involves walking under the hot sun, and many pilgrims continue walking from the Jamārāt to the Ḥaram (Ka'bah) due to the difficulty of finding transportation in the massive crowds. This physical endurance is a key aspect of the *Ḥajj* experience.

Even the act of completing the *sa'y*, walking between the hills of *Ṣafā* and *Marwah* seven times, covers approximately 3.5 kilometres, with the two hills being 400–500 metres apart. Then there is the *tawāf*, the circling of the Ka'bah seven times. On the ground floor, each *tawāf* spans around 75–80 metres, meaning seven circuits total approximately 525–600 metres, about half a kilometre. However, due to the large crowds, many pilgrims perform *tawāf* on higher levels, where the distance increases significantly, reaching about 2.5 kilometres on the top floor. This means that *Ḥajj* involves a substantial amount of walking, often under intense heat, in overcrowded conditions, or both. Completing these physically demanding rituals requires not only physical resilience but also significant mental strength and perseverance.

This physical activity during *Ḥajj* highlights Islām's emphasis on physical well-being. The demanding nature of these rituals signals that such physical exertion is not just a one-time experience but should ideally be part of a Muslim's everyday life. While there are concessions for those unable to walk long distances due to health or age, these are exceptions rather than the norm. The physical endurance required in *Ḥajj* reflects the importance Islām places on maintaining physical fitness and therefore the importance of making physical activity an integral part of a balanced life.

Leaving everything behind for an extended period requires significant mental strength. Pilgrims must part with their families, homes, work, and the routines that define their daily lives. For many, this may be their first experience of such separation, making it emotionally and mentally challenging. Coping with this detachment from their "possessions" requires resilience, as they focus on worship while being distant from the comfort and familiarity of their usual surroundings. This experience fosters mental fortitude, teaching pilgrims to prioritise spiritual devotion over worldly attachments, which helps to build inner strength and clarity.

Social Cohesion

Research has shown that Muslim communities become more open after the *Ḥajj* experience. A study found that the *Ḥajj* experience promotes peaceful coexistence, equality, and harmony. Specifically, *Ḥajj* increases belief in equality and harmony among ethnic groups and the Muslim community. Those who go to *Ḥajj* also "show increased belief in peace, and in equality and harmony among adherents of different religions" (Clingingsmith, Khwaja & Kremer, 2009, p. 1133).

The *Ḥajj* experience fosters a sense of global unity among Muslims. Pilgrims return with a heightened awareness of the diversity within the Muslim *ummah* and a stronger connection to Muslims from various cultural and ethnic backgrounds. This exposure to a multitude of different traditions within the framework of Islām encourages a broader, more inclusive worldview. Additionally, the communal aspects of *Ḥajj*, where people from all walks of life perform rituals side by side, reinforce the values of humility and equality, bridging social and economic divides that may exist prior to the pilgrimage. This heightened sense of unity and shared purpose not only contributes to a more tolerant and cohesive Muslim community post-*Ḥajj* but also a more cohesive community within all walks of life.

Conclusion

Ṣawm and *Ḥajj* are not merely acts of worship; they are transformative practices that holistically enhance a Muslim's well-being. Fasting during Ramaḍān fosters self-discipline, gratitude, and empathy, while also promoting mental, emotional, and physical health. *Ḥajj*, with its spiritually and physically demanding rituals, strengthens mental resilience, promotes global unity among Muslims, and cultivates a profound sense of equality. Both *Ṣawm* and *Ḥajj* are powerful means to attain spiritual growth and emotional balance.

Overall, the five pillars of Islām serve as essential acts of worship that guide a Muslim's life spiritually, mentally, emotionally, physically, and socially. They form a comprehensive framework that fosters a deep connection with Allāh, promoting personal development, self-discipline, and emotional resilience. By engaging in these practices, Muslims are not only working towards their spiritual growth but also improving their mental well-being while contributing to a more just and cohesive society. Each pillar facilitates detachments from worldly matters which can be an obstacle to a strong connection with Allāh. Ultimately, the five pillars represent the foundation of a balanced and fulfilling life in this world, while preparing believers for the eternal rewards of the afterlife.

References

Bukhârî. In-book reference: Book 25, Hadith 8. English translation: Vol. 2, Book 26, Hadith 596. https://sunnah.com/bukhari:1521.

Clingingsmith, D., Khwaja, A. I., & Kremer, M. (2009). Estimating the impact of the Hajj: Religion and tolerance in Islam's global gathering. *The Quarterly Journal of Economics*, *124*(3), 1133–1170. https://doi.org/10.1162/qjec.2009.124.3.1133.

Coleman, D. (2006). *Emotional intelligence: Why it can matter more than IQ*. Random House Publishing Group.

Fond, G., MacGregor, A., Leboyer, M., & Michalsen, A. (2013). Fasting in mood disorders: Neurobiology and effectiveness. *European Psychiatry*, *28*(1), 1–6.

Ghazzālī, A. H. (1992). *The mysteries of fasting*. Sh. Muhammad Ashraf Publishers.

Ibn Mājah. In-book reference: Book 7, Hadith 109. English translation: Vol. 1, Book 7, Hadith 1746. https://sunnah.com/ibnmajah:1746.

Kul, S., Savaş, E., Öztürk, Z. A., & Karadağ, G. (2014). Does Ramadan fasting alter body weight and blood lipids and fasting blood glucose in a healthy population? A meta-analysis. *Journal of Religion and Health*, *53*(3), 929–942.

Longo, V. D., & Mattson, M. P. (2014). Fasting: Molecular mechanisms and clinical applications. *Cell Metabolism*, *19*(2), 181–192.

Mischel, W. (2014). *The marshmallow test: Understanding self-control and how to master it*. Random House.

Mousavi, S. A., Rezaei, M., Amiri, B. S., & Seifi, M. (2014). Effect of fasting on mental health in the general population of Kermanshah, Iran. *Journal of Fasting and Mental Health*, *2*(2), 65–70.

Muslim (a). In-book reference: Book 13, Hadith 213. English translation: Book 6, Hadith 2567. https://sunnah.com/muslim:1151e.

Muslim (b). In-book reference: Book 53, Hadith 75. English translation: Book 40, Hadith 6852. https://sunnah.com/muslim:2864.

Norouzy, A., Salehi, M., Philippou, E., Arabi, H., Shiva, F., Mehrnoosh, S., & Larijani, B. (2013). Effect of fasting in Ramadan on body composition and nutritional intake: A prospective study. *Journal of Human Nutrition and Dietetics*, *26*(S1), 97–104.
Nursi, S. (1995). *The flashes collection* (Ş. Vahide, Trans.). Sözler.
Nursi, S. (2001). *The letters* (Ş. Vahide, Trans.). Sözler.
Sadeghi, M. S., & Mazaheri, M. A. (2005). The effect of fasting on mental health. *Journal of Psychology*, *35*(3), 292–309.

5 Qur'ânic Spiritual Concepts of *Ikhlāṣ* and *Tawakkul*

Introduction

The Qur'ân presents numerous spiritual concepts that serve as valuable tools for navigating life, offering guidance and direction for everyday life experiences. The strong connection between these Qur'ânic principles and psychological well-being lies in Islām's holistic approach to the human condition. The Qur'ânic spiritual concepts help individuals realise their potential as servants of Allāh by fostering a *Tawḥīd*-centric worldview, one that transcends this worldly existence and keeps the afterlife in focus. Yet, this perspective does not come at the expense of happiness in this life. Instead, Islām provides mechanisms for both spiritual and psychological growth, cultivating resilience and promoting overall well-being, including better mental health. This chapter will focus on two Qur'ânic spiritual concepts: *ikhlāṣ* and *tawakkul*. Chapter 6 will focus on *du'ā'*, *dhikr*, and *tafakkur*. Chapter 7 will cover *ṣabr*, *shukr*, and *istiqāmah*, and finally, Chapter 8 will look at *tawbah*, *istighfār*, *riḍā*, *sakīna*, and *iṭmīnān*.

Ikhlāṣ (Sincerity)

Ikhlāṣ stems from the triliteral root khā lām ṣād (خ ل ص). This root word occurs in 17 Chapters and appears 31 times in the Qur'ân, in six derived forms. *Ikhlāṣ* literally means to purify, refine, and cleanse by removing impurities that lessen value. In Islāmic terminology, it refers to the purification of one's worship and good deeds from any trace of ostentation, pretence, or self-interest, ensuring that all acts are performed solely for the sake of Allāh (Van Donzel, 1998). *Ikhlāṣ* has theological implications as it implies a Muslim performs their religious duties with the awareness of being in the sight of Allāh alone and not for the approval or recognition of others (Adamec, 2016, p. 200). *Ikhlāṣ* can be better understood by examining its opposites: *riyā* and *nifāq*. *Riyā* refers to the act of showing off or pretending in front of others, while *nifāq* denotes hypocrisy. Both behaviours indicate that a person's actions are not for the sake of Allāh but rather for the approval or admiration of people (Murata & Chittick, 2015). These traits undermine sincerity and

DOI: 10.4324/9781003494614-5

corrupt the purity of one's worship, highlighting the critical importance of *ikhlāṣ* in maintaining devotion solely to Allāh rather than contaminating one's actions by seeking benefits or rewards from others.

Ostentation, or *riyā*, can gradually lead to *nifāq*, where certain acts of worship are performed not out of genuine devotion but to gain others' trust, which can then be exploited for personal gain (Yusuf, 2011). In such cases, actions, or even worship, are not done with the heart to please Allāh but instead for other worldly benefits. This leads to misalignment between one's inner world and what one manifests in the outer world, leading to hypocrisy.

Ikhlāṣ is such an important protective state that Satan cannot harm those who have *ikhlāṣ*:

قَالَ رَبِّ بِمَآ أَغْوَيْتَنِى لَأُزَيِّنَنَّ لَهُمْ فِى ٱلْأَرْضِ وَلَأُغْوِيَنَّهُمْ أَجْمَعِينَ
إِلَّا عِبَادَكَ مِنْهُمُ ٱلْمُخْلَصِينَ
قَالَ هَٰذَا صِرَٰطٌ عَلَىَّ مُسْتَقِيمٌ

- *[Iblis] said, "My Lord, because You have put me in error, I will surely make [disobedience] attractive to them on earth, and I will mislead them all, Except Your servants from among them, endowed with sincerity (mukhlisīn) in faith and Your worship." (Allāh) said: "This (path of sincerity in faith) is a straight path (mustaqīm) that I have taken upon Myself (to lead to Me)."*

(Al-Ḥijr, 15:39–41,
interpretation of the meaning)

Sincerity is fundamentally an act of the heart, as it is rooted in the intention behind every action. The well-known hādīth, "Verily, actions are judged by intentions, and every person will have only what they intended" (Bukhâri (a)), emphasises the crucial role of intention in any deed. It is not the outward act itself, but the intention within the heart that holds primary importance. This point beautifully aligns with the *ḥadīth*, "Verily, Allāh does not look at your appearance or wealth, but rather He looks at your hearts and actions" (Muslim). The mention of the heart before actions emphasises that the heart, where intentions reside, takes precedence over the actions themselves.

Ultimately, *ikhlāṣ* is the human embodiment of *Tawhîd*, the absolute devotion to Allāh alone. It is the state where all of one's faith, actions, and intentions are directed solely towards Allāh, acknowledging Him as the One True God. This understanding encompasses the recognition that everything else is creation, wholly dependent on Allāh's will and power. With this realisation, there naturally arises a deep inclination to intend all actions for Allāh alone, as He is the sole source of power and authority over all things. Furthermore, since He is the Creator and the Provider of all the blessings, He is the only One who is worthy of seeking the pleasure of.

Ikhlāṣ (sincerity) is performing all actions solely for the sake of Allāh. Adopting this mindset, and heartset, helps one to avoid being disheartened by reducing expectations from imperfect humans who can often disappoint due to their limitations. It also enhances reliance (*tawakkul*) on Allāh. Since Allāh is the All-Hearing, All-Seeing, All-Powerful, and the Lord (Rabb), He is the most deserving of sincere actions. He is the Perfect One who knows all that one does, feels, and intends. He is also The Appreciative, so no goodness goes unnoticed:

وَمَن تَطَوَّعَ خَيْرًا فَإِنَّ ٱللَّهَ شَاكِرٌ عَلِيمٌ

- *And whoever volunteers good – then indeed, Allāh is appreciative and Knowing.*

(Al-Baqarah, 2:158,
interpretation of the meaning)

Mental Health Benefits of ikhlāṣ

Ikhlāṣ (sincerity) provides significant mental health benefits by reducing expectations from others while also being less affected by their judgements. When individuals act with sincere intentions, free from the desire for recognition or approval from others, they experience reduced pressure and anxiety. This is because *ikhlāṣ* shifts focus from external validation to a sense of internal fulfilment and spiritual contentment. Research on intrinsic motivation shows that when individuals act from a place of sincerity, they tend to have greater emotional resilience and life satisfaction, as they are less affected by external judgements (Deci & Ryan, 2000). *Ikhlāṣ* takes intrinsic motivation one step further as it is fuelled by seeking to gain Divine pleasure. *Ikhlāṣ* also fosters a deep trust in Allāh's plan rather than fully relying on one's self. This leads to greater mental peace, helping individuals navigate life's challenges with more emotional balance.

Additionally, *ikhlāṣ* enhances psychological well-being by aligning one's actions with their values and faith. This alignment promotes a sense of authenticity and reduces cognitive dissonance, a state of inner conflict that arises when actions contradict beliefs (Festinger, 1957). Acting sincerely, with a pure heart and intention, helps individuals avoid feelings of hypocrisy, which can lead to guilt or anxiety. By cultivating *ikhlāṣ*, individuals maintain a clear conscience, leading to greater mental tranquillity. Studies on self-concordance and value-congruent behaviour suggest that individuals who act consistently with their values tend to experience greater psychological well-being (Sangeorzan et al., 2024). In summary, *ikhlāṣ* plays a crucial role in fostering both spiritual and mental health through sincerity of intention, whereby actions are undertaken for the pleasure of Allāh, which means alignment with personal and spiritual values.

Tawakkul (Trust in Allah)

حَسْبِىَ ٱللَّهُ لَآ إِلَـٰهَ إِلَّا هُوَ ۖ عَلَيْهِ تَوَكَّلْتُ

- *Allāh is sufficient for me. There is no god except Him. In Him I put my trust.*

(At-Tawbah, 9:129,
interpretation of the meaning)

Tawakkul stems from the triliteral root wāw kāf lām (و ك ل). This root word occurs in 29 Chapters and appears 70 times in the Qur'ân, in four derived forms. *Tawakkul*, or trust in Allāh, involves entrusting all aspects of one's life to Him while recognising the need to balance human effort and reliance on Divine Will. This principle emphasises using one's abilities and knowledge to make informed decisions, while acknowledging the inherent limitations of human capacity. Although *tawakkul* is a psychological coping mechanism, it is more than that (Rassool, 2023), and it has a strong spiritual component which provides the psychological benefits that it does. Allāh states in the Qur'ân:

فَإِذَا عَزَمْتَ فَتَوَكَّلْ عَلَى ٱللَّهِ ۚ إِنَّ ٱللَّهَ يُحِبُّ ٱلْمُتَوَكِّلِينَ

- *Once you make a decision, put your trust in Allāh. Surely Allāh loves those who trust in Him.*

(Āl ʿImrān, 3:159,
interpretation of the meaning)

This verse highlights the importance of decision-making as part of *tawakkul*, with the key being not to rely solely on oneself for the outcome but to place ultimate trust in Allāh.

Considering human limitations, the discerning individual is prompted to identify and designate the most fitting trustee for the governance of their life. That trustee can be none other than Allāh, Al-Wakīl, denoting the ultimate Trustee. This is beautifully alluded to by Yaqub (pbuh) to his sons when he says:

وَمَآ أُغْنِى عَنكُم مِّنَ ٱللَّهِ مِن شَىْءٍ ۖ إِنِ ٱلْحُكْمُ إِلَّا لِلَّهِ ۖ عَلَيْهِ تَوَكَّلْتُ ۖ وَعَلَيْهِ فَلْيَتَوَكَّلِ ٱلْمُتَوَكِّلُونَ

- *I cannot help you against (what is destined by) Allāh in the least. It is only Allāh Who decides. In Him I put my trust. And in Him let the faithful put their trust.*

(Yūsuf, 12:67,
interpretation of the meaning)

Trusting in Allāh, termed *tawakkul*, emerges organically as the logical and inevitable consequence of truly knowing one's self and knowing Allāh. There is no One free from limitations other than Allāh, the Al-Wakīl (The Trustee). Thus, entrusting one's affairs to Allāh is not merely a prescriptive directive, it is a natural outcome founded on the absolute belief that Allāh is the ultimate Trustee.

قُل لَّن يُصِيبَنَآ إِلَّا مَا كَتَبَ ٱللَّهُ لَنَا هُوَ مَوْلَىٰنَا ۚ وَعَلَى ٱللَّهِ فَلْيَتَوَكَّلِ ٱلْمُؤْمِنُونَ

- *Say, "Nothing will ever befall us except what Allāh has destined for us. He is our Protector." So, in Allāh let the believers put their trust.*

(At-Tawbah, 9:51, interpretation of the meaning)

Ibn Al-Qayyim (2020) eloquently describes *tawakkul* as constituting half of the religion, with the other half being turning to Allāh in repentance and devotion. He explains, "The religion is seeking help and offering worship. Trust is the seeking of help, and turning to God in repentance is worship" (p. 412). This insight highlights the deep interconnection between relying on Allāh and worshipping Him. *Tawakkul* involves entrusting one's affairs to Allāh and seeking His assistance, while repentance represents the continuous return to Allāh in humility and devotion, reflecting the essence of worship. Together, these two aspects form the core of a believer's spiritual journey, guiding them in their relationship with the Divine.

To truly grasp the concept of *tawakkul*, one must first understand and internalise the name of Allāh, Al-Wakīl (The Trustee). Without a deep awareness of the attributes of The Trustee, it is difficult to fully entrust one's affairs to Him. Knowing and reflecting on Allāh's qualities as Al-Wakīl enables a believer to place complete trust in His wisdom, power, and knowledge.

Al-Wakīl is one of the names of Allāh mentioned in the Qur'ân, which can be translated to mean "The Trustee" or "The Disposer of Affairs." The term Wakīl denotes someone who is entrusted with the responsibility of managing the affairs or representing someone else. In the context of Allāh, Al-Wakīl signifies His attribute of being the ultimate trustee and manager of affairs for everyone and everything in the universe. Allāh is relied upon by His creation to manage their affairs, and He is entrusted with the responsibility of safeguarding and overseeing all matters. This Divine name emphasises Allāh's role as the ultimate guardian, protector, and caretaker of His creation. Allāh states in the Qur'ân:

لَّهُۥ مَا فِى ٱلسَّمَـٰوَٰتِ وَمَا فِى ٱلْأَرْضِ ۗ وَكَفَىٰ بِٱللَّهِ وَكِيلًا

- *To Him belongs whatever is in the heavens and whatever is on the earth. And sufficient is Allāh as Disposer of affairs (Wakīl).*

(An-Nisā', 4:171, interpretation of the meaning)

In this verse, Allāh first reminds humanity that everything belongs to Him, everything. This serves as a crucial pretext for understanding and accepting Allāh as Al-Wakīl, for there must be a recognition of the Trustee's capabilities for one to place trust in Him. In another verse, Allāh reiterates that He is sufficient as a Trustee:

حَسْبُنَا ٱللَّهُ وَنِعْمَ ٱلْوَكِيلُ

- *Allāh is sufficient for us and is the best of Disposer of Affairs (Wakīl).*

(Āl ʿImrān, 3:173,
interpretation of the meaning)

As indicated in this Qur'ânic verse, when one places their trust in Allāh, there is no need to rely on anyone else to manage their affairs. Al-Ghazzali refers to Allāh as the absolute Al-Wakīl, the ultimate Trustee, while acknowledging the existence of relative trustees in one's life (Al-Ghazzālī, 2011). These relative trustees may competently fulfil the tasks entrusted to them, but there is always a risk of shortcomings. For instance, someone might entrust their finances to a trustee with financial expertise. However, there are no absolute guarantees that this trustee will make and execute decisions perfectly, as many factors are beyond their control. In contrast, Ghazzali emphasises that Allāh, as the absolute Al-Wakīl, is "the one to whom the matters are entrusted, the one who is conscientious in dealing with them, and the one who is faithful in carrying them out. That one is God Most High alone" (Al-Ghazzālī, 2011, p. 99).

Entrusting one's affairs to others can be difficult, especially when past experiences have eroded trust. However, placing trust in Allāh is fundamentally different from relying on human beings. Allāh is Al-Wakīl, the ultimate Trustee, Whose care is flawless and Whose wisdom is unmatched. Unlike people, who are limited in power and knowledge, Allāh is both Al-Qādir (All-Powerful) and Al-Ḥakīm (All-Wise). A true Trustee must possess the ability to ensure the best possible outcome. Without such power, trust is futile. In the Qur'ân, Allāh affirms His limitless power:

إِنَّمَا أَمْرُهُ إِذَا أَرَادَ شَيْئًا أَن يَقُولَ لَهُ كُن فَيَكُونُ

- *His command, when He intends a thing, is only that He says to it, "Be," and it is.*

(Yā-Sīn, 36:82,
interpretation of the meaning)

However, such power is always exercised with wisdom. Without wisdom, power can become tyrannical, as seen in dictators or narcissists who may possess strength but lack justice, compassion, generosity, and other essential qualities that stem from wisdom. Allāh's wisdom is all-encompassing and flawless. The Qur'ân affirms this:

إِنَّهُۥ هُوَ ٱلْعَلِيمُ ٱلْحَكِيمُ

- *Indeed, it is He who is the Knowing, the Wise.*

(Yūsuf, 12:100,
interpretation of the meaning)

It is Allāh's perfect wisdom that makes entrusting one's affairs to Him so comforting and reassuring, allowing a believer to always place absolute trust in Allāh. Thus, it only makes sense to put your trust in the One who qualifies:

رَّبُّ ٱلْمَشْرِقِ وَٱلْمَغْرِبِ لَآ إِلَـٰهَ إِلَّا هُوَ فَٱتَّخِذْهُ وَكِيلًا

- *(He is) the Lord of the East and the West; there is no deity except Him, so take Him as Disposer of [your] affairs.*

(Al-Muzzammil, 73:9,
interpretation of the meaning)

Process of tawakkul

The practice of *tawakkul* is not easily navigated, especially in a world governed by cause and effect. *Tawakkul* does not mean passively waiting for results without effort, nor does it absolve one from taking responsibility for their decisions. Rather, it involves making thoughtful decisions, taking the necessary actions, and then placing trust in Allāh for the outcome:

فَإِذَا عَزَمْتَ فَتَوَكَّلْ عَلَى ٱللَّهِ

- *Once you make a decision, put your trust in Allāh.*

(Āl ʿImrān, 3:159,
interpretation of the meaning)

Regarding taking responsibility for one's actions, the Prophet Muḥammad ﷺ was asked whether a person should tie their camel and trust in Allāh, or leave it untied and trust in Allāh. The Prophet replied, "Tie her and trust in Allāh" (Tirmidhī). This highlights that while trust in Allāh is essential, one must also exert their utmost effort in striving for an outcome before entrusting it to Him. That is, one must always tie their camel, as best as they can.

Ultimately, for a believer, taking action is an acknowledgement that, while they possess the intellect to make judgements and decisions, they do not have the power to determine the results. For example, in the case of tying a camel, a believer understands that tying the camel should, in theory, prevent it from escaping. However, they cannot control whether this will mean the safe keeping of the camel. Someone could cut the rope, the knot may not be tied securely enough, or the camel might remain tied but later die from illness. In the latter scenario, although the camel remains tied, it is still lost. This illustrates that while a believer's efforts are necessary, the ultimate outcome is beyond their control and rests with Allāh.

In today's world, the camel could represent a car, house, or any other possession. A believer takes all necessary precautions to keep these possessions safe: locking their car after parking or securing their home before leaving. Yet, they do not have the power to guarantee their safety. This is where a believer entrusts their possessions to Allāh, for He alone has the power to protect them, should He choose to do so, based on His infinite Power and Wisdom.

Tawakkul is not limited to possessions but also applies to decisions. Just as tying the camel represents taking responsible action, it also symbolises making the best decision possible and then entrusting the outcome to Allāh, as humans cannot control results. Whether one chooses to marry, travel, work, or pursue other tasks, they do so with specific intentions and take steps towards fulfilling those choices. The crucial point to understand is that the outcome is not within their control, it is in the hands of Allāh, the Causer of Causes.

Mental Health Benefits of tawakkul

Tawakkul, or placing trust in Allāh, plays a significant role in enhancing mental well-being by fostering a sense of peace and contentment. When individuals embrace *tawakkul*, they relinquish excessive worry and anxiety, acknowledging that the outcome of their efforts is ultimately in Allāh's hands. According to Gondal et al. (2022),

> Individuals who are sincere with their religion i.e., who have intrinsic religious orientation may have a high degree of tawakkul, which in turn may protect them from developing symptoms of mental health issues.
>
> (p. 42)

This reliance on Divine Wisdom reduces the burden of constant stress and fear of the unknown, promoting emotional calmness. Studies in positive psychology highlight that trust in a higher power is correlated with reduced anxiety and better coping mechanisms in stressful situations (Koenig, 2012). The Qur'ân supports this, reinforcing the idea that faith can act as a powerful source of mental peace and therefore mental health.

Conclusion

Both *ikhlāṣ* and *tawakkul* offer spiritual and psychological benefits that contribute to an individual's overall well-being. *Ikhlāṣ* fosters sincerity in one's intentions, reducing the stress and anxiety that come from seeking external validation, while enhancing authenticity and alignment with personal and spiritual values. *Tawakkul*, however, brings emotional peace and resilience by allowing believers to place their trust in Allāh, relieving them of the burden of trying to control outcomes. Together, these two concepts promote a balanced approach to life, where one actively engages in the world with faith while also being conscious of the afterlife.

References

Adamec, L. W. (2016). *Historical dictionary of Islam*. Rowman & Littlefield.

Bukhârî. In-book reference: Book 83, Hadith 66. English translation: Vol. 8, Book 78, Hadith 680. https://sunnah.com/bukhari:6689.

Deci, E. L., & Ryan, R. M. (2000). The "what" and "why" of goal pursuits: Human needs and the self-determination of behavior. *Psychological Inquiry*, *11*(4), 227–268.

Festinger, L. (1957). *A theory of cognitive dissonance*. Stanford University Press.

Al-Ghazzālī, A. H. (2011). *The ninety-nine beautiful names of God*. Islamic Texts Society.

Gondal, M. U., Adil, A., & Niazi, S. (2022). Tawakkul mediates between religious orientation and depression among Muslims. *Clinical and Counselling Psychology Review*, *3*(2), 26–45. https://doi.org/10.32350/ccpr.32.02.

Ibn Qayyim. (2020). *Madarij al-Salikin* [The ranks of the divine seekers] (O. Ajum, Trans.). Brill.

Koenig, H. G. (2012). *Religion, spirituality, and health: The research and clinical implications*. ISRN Psychiatry.

Murata, S., & Chittick, W. C. (2015). *The vision of Islam*. Paragon House.

Muslim. In-book reference: Book 45, Hadith 42. English translation: Book 32, Hadith 6221. https://sunnah.com/muslim:2564c.

Rassool, G. H. (2023). Critical reflections on current status of scholarship in Islamic psychology – Challenges and solutions. *Australian Journal of Islamic Studies*, *8*(3), 37–54.

Sangeorzan, P. C., Goodson, W. L., & Bohon, L. M. (2024). The why to bear any how: Goal self-concordance, meaning, and depressive and anxious symptomatology. *International Journal of Applied Positive Psychology*, *9*(2), 879–898.

Tirmidhī. In-book reference: Book 37, Hadith 103. English translation: Vol. 4, Book 11, Hadith 2517. https://sunnah.com/tirmidhi:2517.

Van Donzel, E. (1998). *The encyclopaedia of Islam:* New edition (Vol. 21). E.J. Brill.

Yusuf, H. (2011). *Purification of the heart: Signs, symptoms, and cures of the spiritual diseases of the heart*. Starlatch.

6 Qur'ânic Spiritual Concepts of *Du'ā'*, *Dhikr*, and *Tafakkur*

Introduction

This chapter continues the discussion of Qur'ânic spiritual concepts that serve as valuable tools for navigating life, offering guidance and direction for everyday life experiences. *Du'ā'* (supplication), *dhikr* (remembrance of Allāh), and *tafakkur* (reflection) are important spiritual practices deeply rooted in the Qur'ân and Islāmic tradition. These concepts serve as essential tools for fostering both spiritual and mental well-being, offering believers guidance and strength in navigating the complexities of life. *Du'ā'* allows for an intimate dialogue with Allāh, where believers can express their deepest concerns, seek help, and find solace from the One who hears all. *Dhikr* keeps the heart constantly connected to Allāh, providing inner peace and resilience. *Tafakkur* encourages deep reflection on creation and life's purpose, enhancing mindfulness and spiritual growth. Each and every one of these practices contribute towards spiritual and psychological well-being.

Du'ā' (Supplication)

وَإِذَا سَأَلَكَ عِبَادِي عَنِّي فَإِنِّي قَرِيبٌ ۖ أُجِيبُ دَعْوَةَ الدَّاعِ إِذَا دَعَانِ

- *And when (O Messenger) My servants ask you about Me, then surely, I am near. I answer the prayer of the supplicant when he prays to Me...*

(Al-Baqarah, 2:186, interpretation of the meaning)

Du'ā' stems from the triliteral root dāl 'ayn wāw (د ع و). This root word occurs in 55 Chapters and appears 212 times in the Qur'ân, in four derived forms. *Du'ā'* literally means to call out, to invoke, to request, to ask for help. According to Islāmic literature, it describes the state of a person admitting their weakness before Allāh's Might and Power and with love and respect, requesting Allāh's blessings and His help. *Du'ā'* is a personal calling upon Allāh (Murata & Chittick, 2015). It is an informal prayer in which one asks the Creator for

DOI: 10.4324/9781003494614-6

"what they want in their own words or according to formulas set by Prophet Muḥammad ﷺ or the Qur'ân" (Abdullah, 2003, p. 68).

Du'ā' can be understood as a personal conversation between the servant and Allāh. It transcends the formal rituals of worship, embodying a direct and personal connection with one's Creator. When *du'ā'* is described as a personal conversation, the intimate nature of *du'ā'* is highlighted. Unlike formal prayers (*ṣalāh*), which follow specific guidelines and are recited at set times, *du'ā'* can be made at any time, in any place, and in any language. It is a spontaneous and sincere expression of the heart's desires, concerns, and gratitude. In this way, *du'ā'* reflects the closeness and accessibility of Allāh to His servants. In Chapter 2 verse 186 of the Qur'ân, Allāh uses personal language rather than majestic pronouns such as "we" or "us":

وَإِذَا سَأَلَكَ عِبَادِى عَنِّى فَإِنِّى قَرِيبٌ أُجِيبُ دَعْوَةَ ٱلدَّاعِ إِذَا دَعَانِ

- *And when (O Messenger) My servants ask you about Me, then surely, I am near. I answer the prayer of the supplicant when he prays to Me...*

(Al-Baqarah, 2:186,
interpretation of the meaning)

This personal conversation is not restricted by time or space, allowing the believer to express their thoughts, needs, and emotions freely. It is a moment where the barriers between the earthly and the Divine are reduced, allowing for a pure, heartfelt dialogue. The believer may ask for guidance, seek forgiveness, express fears, or simply pour out their heart, knowing that Allāh is always listening. Through *du'ā'*, a believer fulfils their purpose of creation and realises their true worth:

قُلْ مَا يَعْبَؤُا۟ بِكُمْ رَبِّى لَوْلَا دُعَآؤُكُمْ

- *Say, "What would my Lord care for you if not for your supplication?"*

(Al-Furqān, 25:77,
interpretation of the meaning)

Du'ā' attracts Allāh's mercy and compassion upon the supplicant, as it acknowledges Allāh's lordship, power, and ability to respond. In making *du'ā'*, one recognises Allāh's sovereignty and His absolute capacity to bring about change, reinforcing the believer's dependence on Him. *Du'ā'* is an expression of humility before one's Creator. It acts as a powerful means to subdue the carnal *nafs* (ego), which often craves control and power. Through *du'ā'*, the *nafs* is reminded that it neither has full control nor possesses true power; that authority belongs solely to Allāh. In the Qur'ân, Allāh underscores this by stating,

دَاخِرِينَ وَقَالَ رَبُّكُمُ ٱدْعُونِىٓ أَسْتَجِبْ لَكُمْ إِنَّ ٱلَّذِي ن يَسْتَكْبِرُونَ عَنْ عِبَادَتِى سَيَدْخُلُونَ جَهَنَّ م

- *Call upon Me; I will respond to you. Indeed, those who are too proud to worship Me will enter Hell in humiliation.*

(Ghāfir, 40:60,
interpretation of the meaning)

This verse highlights the necessity of surrendering to Allāh, rather than being arrogant, by recognising the need for Allāh's assistance. The same point is echoed in the *ḥadīth*: "Indeed, he who does not ask Allāh, He (Allāh) gets angry with him" (Tirmidhî). Not asking from Allāh when in need reflects an underlying pride, implying a belief that one does not need Him and that one can manage their own affairs, an attitude far from the reality of human dependence on Allāh.

Through *du'ā'*, a believer deeply experiences their servanthood, aligning with their *fiṭrah*, their innate nature. *Du'ā'* holds important positive implications, serving as an acknowledgment of the existence of the One God who possesses power over all things. In making *du'ā'*, a believer becomes acutely aware of Allāh's closeness, His ability to hear, and His power to respond to prayers. It reflects a heightened consciousness of one's role as a servant, breaking through *ghaflah* (heedlessness), even if momentarily. *Du'ā'* signifies a recognition of limitations and weaknesses in contrast to the immense greatness of Allāh. It is a demonstration of respect, trust, and reliance on Allāh, as the believer lays bare their innermost thoughts, seeking forgiveness and asking for help in all matters.

Mental Health Benefits of Du'ā'

Making *du'ā'* offers incredible mental health benefits, acting as both a spiritual and psychological coping mechanism. From an Islāmic perspective, *du'ā'* serves as a direct communication with Allāh, fostering a sense of reliance, hope, and peace during challenging times. To understand the benefits of *du'ā'*, Yucel undertook research to "investigate the physical and spiritual effects of prayer on Muslim patients" in hospital (Yucel, 2010, p. 45). The results from the research showed that patients who made *du'ā'* were more hopeful and confident while having lesser symptoms of depression, anxiety, loneliness, and despair (Yucel, 2010).

From a psychological viewpoint, *du'ā'* can be likened to cognitive-behavioural interventions where individuals release control over uncontrollable aspects of their lives. By verbalising concerns and seeking Divine assistance, individuals often experience a release of burdens, akin to practices of journaling or talk therapy.

Hope is also a key component of *du'ā'*. Charles Snyder, a leading positive psychologist, states that hope has two necessary elements to it; "perception of successful agency related to goals" and "perceived availability of successful pathways" (Snyder et al., 1991, p. 570). In other words, one needs to believe a goal can be achieved while also believing that there is a pathway to achieve that goal. Belief in Allāh and making *du'ā'* provides these two elements because a believer has the conviction that anything is possible for Allāh, making goals achievable, through the pathway of asking of Allāh. Thus, *du'ā'* serves as an invaluable tool for promoting mental health by providing both psychological comfort and spiritual fulfilment.

Dhikr (Remembrance of Allāh)

أَلَا بِذِكْرِ ٱللَّهِ تَطْمَئِنُّ ٱلْقُلُوبُ

- *Surely in the remembrance of Allāh do hearts find rest.*

(Ar-Ra'd, 13:28,
interpretation of the meaning)

Dhikr stems from the triliteral root dhāl kāf rā (ذ ك ر). This root word occurs in 71 Chapters and appears 292 times in the Qur'ân, in 11 derived forms. In its most literal sense, *dhikr* means to mention or remember something, involving the act of recollection or citing. In the Islāmic context, it is defined as "recollection, remembrance, reminiscence, commemoration, naming, mentioning, invocation of Allah, mention of the Lord's Name" (Wehr, 1979, p. 153). Thus, any form of remembrance of Allāh, in any manner, is considered *dhikr*. As Unal (2015) explains,

> Dhikr encompasses all words of praise and glorification of Allāh. Additionally, reading, reflecting, studying to gain knowledge of Allāh, and speaking about Him to others are also included within the concept of dhikr. (p. 877)

Thus, *dhikr* can be understood in three basic senses: mentioning, remembering, and reminding. To mention something with the tongue is to recall it to the mind, which constitutes remembering. If others are present, they are simultaneously being reminded (Murata & Chittick, 2015). *Dhikr* serves as a means to bring Allāh to the forefront of one's life, occupying both the heart and mind with Him. It is an act of worship that can be performed at any time and place, as the Qur'ân states:

ٱلَّذِينَ يَذْكُرُونَ ٱللَّهَ قِيَٰمًا وَقُعُودًا وَعَلَىٰ جُنُوبِهِمْ وَيَتَفَكَّرُونَ فِى خَلْقِ ٱلسَّمَٰوَٰتِ
وَٱلْأَرْضِ رَبَّنَا مَا خَلَقْتَ هَٰذَا بَٰطِلًا

- *Those who remember Allāh standing, sitting, and lying down, who reflect on the creation of the heavens and earth: "Our Lord! You have not created all this without purpose".*

(Āl 'Imrān, 3:191,
interpretation of the meaning)

In various parts of the Qur'ân, Allāh emphasises that the Qur'ân itself is a reminder:

إِنْ هُوَ إِلَّا ذِكْرٌ وَقُرْءَانٌ مُّبِينٌ

- *This is only a reminder and a Clear Qur'ân.*

(Yā-Sīn, 36:69, interpretation of the meaning)

وَإِنَّهُ لَذِكْرٌ لَّكَ وَلِقَوْمِكَ ۖ وَسَوْفَ تُسْـَٔلُونَ

- *Indeed, it (the Qur'ân) is a reminder for you and for your people, in which lie your honour and happiness (in both worlds).*

(Az-Zukhruf, 43:44, interpretation of the meaning)

As highlighted in the last verse, remembering the Qur'ân is a source of happiness and fulfilment for Muslims in both this life and the Hereafter, for it is a guide and a manual to navigate through every facet of life. The Qur'ân helps to give meaning to life events in a way that soothes the heart while it also provides guidance in making decisions that will benefit this life and the next.

One of the most powerful verses regarding the benefits of remembering Allāh states:

ٱلَّذِينَ ءَامَنُوا۟ وَتَطْمَئِنُّ قُلُوبُهُم بِذِكْرِ ٱللَّهِ ۗ أَلَا بِذِكْرِ ٱللَّهِ تَطْمَئِنُّ ٱلْقُلُوبُ

- *Those who have faith and whose hearts find peace in the remembrance of God. Truly it is in the remembrance of God that hearts find peace.*

(Ar-Ra'd, 13:28, interpretation of the meaning)

Dhikr offers immense benefits for the spiritual heart, serving as the ultimate means to attain peace. This is no surprise since the heart's fundamental purpose is to believe in Allāh. If the heart was created to believe in Allāh, then any practice that reminds the heart of Him naturally aligns with one's *fiṭrah*. *Dhikr* is essentially what the heart was designed to do, so when it engages in this practice, it experiences peace and serenity. That is, there is no tension or conflict between what the heart is seeking and what it is receiving, allowing it to settle into its intended state of harmony. The remembrance of Allāh is so vital that numerous Qur'ânic verses and *ḥadīth* repeatedly emphasise its importance. One such example is:

يَـٰٓأَيُّهَا ٱلَّذِينَ ءَامَنُوا۟ ٱذْكُرُوا۟ ٱللَّهَ ذِكْرًا كَثِيرًا

- *Oh, you who have believed, remember Allāh with much remembrance.*

(Al-Aḥzāb, 33:41, interpretation of the meaning)

The emphasis on plentiful remembrance is worth noting. Just as the physical heart requires a constant supply of oxygen to survive, the spiritual heart similarly depends on a continual supply of *dhikr* to thrive. Without it, the spiritual heart becomes deprived and weakened, and there is an increased risk of it dying. *Dhikr* sustains a spiritually healthy heart by nurturing one's relationship with Allāh, a relationship that Allāh reciprocates, as He says in the Qur'ân,

فَٱذْكُرُونِىٓ أَذْكُرْكُمْ

- *Remember Me, and I will remember you.*

(Al-Baqarah, 2:152,
interpretation of the meaning)

This reciprocal relationship with Allāh deepens through the practice of *dhikr*, as captured beautifully in the following *Ḥadīth* Qudsi:

> Allāh the Exalted says, "I am as My servant expects Me and I am with him as he remembers Me. If he remembers Me in himself, then I will remember him in Myself. If he mentions Me in a gathering, then I will mention him in a greater gathering. When he draws near Me by the span of his hand, I draw near him by the length of a cubit. When he draws near Me by the length of a cubit, I draw near him by the length of a fathom. When he comes to Me walking, I will come to him running."
>
> (Bukhârî)

Dhikr holds great ability to facilitate connection with Allāh. When one reaches out to Allāh through remembering and thinking of Him, Allāh responds manifold, remembering, mentioning, and drawing closer to the believer. This connection brings comfort and solace to the heart, for truly, in the remembrance of Allāh, do hearts find rest.

Mental Health Benefits of Dhikr

Engaging in *dhikr* has been shown to offer substantial mental health benefits, particularly in alleviating stress and anxiety. Regular practice of *dhikr* creates a soothing effect, helping individuals manage symptoms like restlessness, tension, and difficulty concentrating. This sense of inner peace comes from placing trust in Allāh's plan, which is central to the calming nature of *dhikr*.

Hamsyah and Subandi (2017) emphasise the spiritual and psychological cleansing that *dhikr* provides, relieving mental burdens and promoting optimism in life's challenges. It fosters a deeper connection with Allāh, filling individuals with love, happiness, and contentment. Furthermore, *dhikr* helps reduce egoism and arrogance, encouraging humility and gratitude. Research supports the positive effects of *dhikr*, showing, for example, that it significantly lowers academic stress among students (Munjirin et al., 2023) and improves mental health in older adults by nearly doubling their emotional well-being (Anwar et al., 2024). The combination of spiritual and psychological benefits makes *dhikr* a powerful tool for enhancing mental health.

Tafakkur **(Reflection)**

أَوَلَمْ يَتَفَكَّرُوا فِىٓ أَنفُسِهِم

- *Have they not reflected upon their own being?*

(Ar-Rūm, 30:8,
interpretation of the meaning)

Tafakkur stems from the triliteral root *fā kāf rā* (ف ك ر). This root word occurs in 13 Chapters and appears 18 times in the Qur'ân, in two derived forms. *Tafakkur*, a deep process of reflection, meditation, and contemplation, is an important concept in Islām. It refers to the deliberate and mindful use of one's intellect to ponder over the creation, existence, and the signs of Allāh. The terms associated with *tafakkur*, such as cogitate, muse, speculate, and revolve in one's mind, all reflect a deep and sustained engagement with thought, which moves beyond surface-level understanding to a deeper connection with true reality.

When a believer engages in *tafakkur*, they are encouraged to use their mind in a way that unlocks its full potential. As Zarabozo (2002) points out, when the mind is properly engaged, it naturally leads to a recognition of the truth of Allāh's oneness (*Tawhîd*) and fosters a stronger desire to worship Him. This intellectual exercise becomes a pathway not just to knowledge but to spiritual growth and closeness to Allāh. The act of pondering over the universe, the self, and the intricate systems of life inevitably directs the believer towards acknowledging the greatness of the Creator, which ultimately strengthens one's faith.

The connection between *tafakkur*, belief in Allāh, and one's relationship with Him is a key outcome of *tafakkur* because *tafakkur* is not just an intellectual exercise but a form of worship. It is a way to engage with the world and its signs (*āyah*) that Allāh has placed in the creation to guide humankind towards Him. Through deep reflection on these signs, whether they are in nature, in the Qur'ân, or in the events of one's own life, the believer is able to reaffirm their belief in Allāh and draw closer to Him. This connection is not just through passive acceptance but through active engagement with the mind and heart, leading to a closer relationship with Allāh.

While a significant focus of *tafakkur* is connection with Allāh, it is broader than that. Ibn Qayyim states, "When a man is used to contemplation, he will learn a lesson from everything" (Ibn Qayyim, n.d., p. 180). Through *tafakkur*, every observation and every experience can be a source of learning.

However, for this to be achieved, both the *qalb* and *'aql* must be utilised for their intended purpose. This means aligning these faculties with one's *fiṭrah* so that Allāh remains at the centre of all thoughts and decisions. When this is achieved, *tafakkur* becomes second nature that ultimately leads to a better understanding of Allāh and one's purpose in the grand scheme of things:

ٱلَّذِينَ يَذْكُرُونَ ٱللَّهَ قِيَٰمًا وَقُعُودًا وَعَلَىٰ جُنُوبِهِمْ وَيَتَفَكَّرُونَ فِى خَلْقِ ٱلسَّمَٰوَٰتِ
وَٱلْأَرْضِ رَبَّنَا مَا خَلَقْتَ هَٰذَا بَٰطِلًا سُبْحَٰنَكَ فَقِنَا عَذَابَ ٱلنَّارِ

- *They are˺ those who remember (dhikr) Allāh while standing, sitting, and lying on their sides, and reflect (tafakkur) on the creation of the heavens and the earth ˹and pray˺, "Our Lord! You have not created ˹all of˺ this without purpose. Glory be to You! Protect us from the torment of the Fire."*

(Āl ʿImrān, 3:191,
interpretation of the meaning)

Malik Badri elaborates on *tafakkur* as a "a cognitive spiritual activity in which the rational mind, emotion and spirit are combined" (Badri, 2018, p. xii). Thus, *tafakkur* is spiritual in nature, as opposed to Western contemplation. It is a refined form of worshipping Allāh by appreciating His creation in His vast universe. Its ultimately leads to the development of spiritual awareness or remembrance and consciousness of Allāh (*taqwa*).

Thus, *tafakkur* is a vital practice for nurturing and strengthening one's faith. It transforms the believer's understanding of the world, helping them see everything as a sign of Allāh's existence and power. In turn, this deepens their worship and devotion, fostering a continual, reflective connection with their Creator.

Mental Health Benefits of Tafakkur

Tafakkur holds substantial mental health benefits as it encourages mindfulness and self-awareness while keeping Allāh at the centre of this reflective practice. Engaging in *tafakkur* allows individuals to pause and immerse in reflection on themselves (their thoughts, emotions, and behaviours), the universe and the Creator, all the while having a Tawhîd-centric lens. *Tafakkur* is different to mindfulness, with mindfulness being defined as, "the ability to observe thoughts, bodily sensations or feelings in the present moment with an open and accepting orientation toward one's experiences" (Grossman et al., 2004, p. 103). This would be akin to *muraqaba* in the Islāmic tradition. Neither does the Western understanding of meditation or contemplation truly reflect what *tafakkur* is since the aim of *tafakkur* "is necessarily spiritual in nature"

(Badri, 2018, p. xxx). Nevertheless, due to common elements between *tafakkur*, meditation, and contemplation, many of the benefits of meditation and contemplation would manifest in *tafakkur* as well, such as clarity and focus.

Malik Badri's *Contemplation: An Islamic Psychospiritual Study* (2018) explores the psychological and spiritual benefits of *tafakkur* in Islām. Badri emphasises that *tafakkur* is not merely a cognitive process but a deeply spiritual practice that connects individuals to Allāh and enhances mental well-being. *Tafakkur* integrates spirituality with psychology, offering a holistic approach to mental health by balancing rational thought with spiritual introspection to achieve both personal growth and Divine closeness.

Conclusion

Du'ā', *dhikr*, and t*afakkur* are key Qur'ânic spiritual concepts that contribute to spiritual growth and psychological well-being. Through *du'ā'*, believers cultivate a direct, personal relationship with Allāh, reinforcing reliance on His wisdom and power. *Dhikr* offers the constant remembrance that brings peace and stability to the heart, while *tafakkur* encourages reflection, deepening one's understanding of creation and life's purpose. Together, these practices foster a holistic well-being that aligns with the *Tawḥīd*-centric worldview of Islām, helping individuals find balance, resilience, and a sense of purpose in both their spiritual and everyday lives.

References

Abdullah, A. R. (2003). *Healing with the medicine of the Prophet*. Darussalam.

Anwar, S., Siregar, S. M. F., Alamsyah, T., Muliadi, T., Marniati, M., & Khairunnas, K. (2024). The dhikr and the mental health of the elderly in Aceh, Indonesia. *Health SA, SA Gesondheid*, *29*, 2456. https://doi.org/10.4102/hsag.v29i0.2456.

Badri, M. (2018). *Contemplation: An Islamic psychospiritual study*. International Institute of Islamic Thought (IIIT).

Bukhârî. In-book reference: Book 97, Hadith 34. English translation: Vol. 9, Book 93, Hadith 502. https://sunnah.com/tirmidhi/48.

Grossman, P., Heidenreich, T., & Michalak, J. (2004). Mindfulness practice: A unique clinical intervention for the behavioral sciences. *Mindfulness and Acceptance in Psychotherapy*, *1*, 16–18.

Hamsyah, F., & Subandi, M. A. (2017). Dzikir and happiness: A mental health study on an Indonesian Muslim Sufi group. *Journal of Spirituality in Mental Health, 19*(1), 80–94. https://doi.org/10.1080/19349637.2017.1278671.

Ibn Qayyim. (n.d.). *Miftah, dar al-sa'adah*. Riasat al-Ifta.

Munjirin, A., Yustia, F. A., Nurdin, F. N. A., & Assakinah, N. F. (2023). The effectiveness of Dhikr relaxation therapy in reducing level of academic stress among students in the first academic semester of the Islamic Guidance Study Program. *International*

Journal of Research and Innovation in Social Science (IJRISS), 7(12), 251–256. https://doi.org/10.47772/IJRISS.2023.7012021.

Murata, S., & Chittick, W. C. (2015). *The vision of Islam*. Paragon House.

Snyder, C. R., Harris, C., Anderson, J. R., Holleran, S. A., Irving, L. M., & Sigmon, S. T. (1991). The will and the ways: Development and validation of an individual-differences measure of hope. *Journal of Personality and Social Psychology, 60*, 570–585.

Tirmidhî. In-book reference: Book 48, Hadith 4. English translation: Vol. 6, Book 45, Hadith 3373. https://sunnah.com/tirmidhi/48.

Unal, A. (2015). *Living the ethics and morality of Islam*. Işık Yayıncılık Ticaret.

Wehr, H. (1979). *A dictionary of modern written Arabic*. Otto Harrassowitz Verlag.

Yucel, S. (2010). *Prayer and healing in Islam: With addendum of 25 remedies for the sick by Said Nursi*. Tughra Books.

Zarabozo, J. (2002). *Purification of the soul: Concept, process and means*. Al-Basheer Publications & Translations.

7 Qur'ânic Spiritual Concepts of *Ṣabr*, *Shukr*, and *Istiqāmah*

Introduction

This chapter continues the discussion of Qur'ânic spiritual concepts that serve as valuable tools for navigating life, offering guidance and direction for everyday life experiences. The Qur'ânic concepts of *ṣabr* (patience), *shukr* (gratitude), and *istiqāmah* (steadfastness) offer guidance for leading a balanced and resilient life. These psycho-spiritual concepts not only shape a believer's relationship with Allah but also play a crucial role in mental and emotional well-being. *Ṣabr* helps individuals endure life's inevitable challenges with the right mindset and heartset. *Shukr* provides a positive mindset by encouraging gratitude for blessings, which fosters contentment. *Istiqāmah*, or steadfastness, ensures one's faith and actions remain aligned with their spiritual values, promoting consistency and inner peace. Together, these concepts provide a holistic framework for spiritual and psychological growth.

Ṣabr (Patience)

Ṣabr stems from the triliteral root ṣād bā rā (ص ب ر). This root word occurs in 45 Chapters and appears 103 times in the Qur'ân, in six derived forms. *Ṣabr*, literally means to endure, bear, and resist pain, suffering, and difficulty, while remaining calm in the face of problems. It is often translated as patience. However, it can also be understood as steadfastness, perseverance, and endurance (Esposito, 2004). While patience is strongly associated with life's trials, its scope extends far beyond this. Patience is also the virtue that prevents impulsive behaviour and helps one maintain self-control. It ensures that, in moments of challenge or adversity, a person can respond spiritually, physically, emotionally, and mentally in the most appropriate and balanced

DOI: 10.4324/9781003494614-7

manner for the given situation. Allāh commands patience in various Qur'ānic verses, such as:

وَٱسْتَعِينُوا۟ بِٱلصَّبْرِ وَٱلصَّلَوٰةِ

- *Seek help in patience and prayer.*

(Al-Baqarah, 2:45,
interpretation of the meaning)

يَـٰٓأَيُّهَا ٱلَّذِينَ ءَامَنُوا۟ ٱصْبِرُوا۟ وَصَابِرُوا۟ وَرَابِطُوا۟ وَٱتَّقُوا۟ ٱللَّهَ لَعَلَّكُمْ تُفْلِحُونَ

- *O believers! Patiently endure, persevere, stand on guard, and be mindful of Allah, so you may be successful.*

(Āl 'Imrān, 3:200,
interpretation of the meaning)

Patience is not merely a recommended response but a necessity, especially in times of hardship. The Qur'ân exalts those who embody patience, praising them with statements such as:

إِنَّا وَجَدْنَـٰهُ صَابِرًا ۚ نِّعْمَ ٱلْعَبْدُ ۖ إِنَّهُۥٓ أَوَّابٌ

- ... *We truly found him patient. What an excellent servant! Indeed, he constantly turned to Allāh.*

(Ṣād, 38:44,
interpretation of the meaning)

Numerous verses highlight the significance of patience, praising the virtue and outlining the rewards for those who maintain it. Moreover, Allāh promises His companionship and closeness to the patient:

يَـٰٓأَيُّهَا ٱلَّذِينَ ءَامَنُوا۟ ٱسْتَعِينُوا۟ بِٱلصَّبْرِ وَٱلصَّلَوٰةِ ۚ إِنَّ ٱللَّهَ مَعَ ٱلصَّـٰبِرِينَ

- *Oh believers! Seek comfort in patience and prayer. Allah is truly with those who are patient.*

(Al-Baqarah, 2:153, interpretation of the meaning)

The consistent message conveyed in both the Qur'ân and *ḥadīth* is that patience is a noble and esteemed quality that draws a person closer to Allāh. It is also a trait that pleases Allāh and for which He promises immense rewards. Prophet Muḥammad ﷺ emphasised the value of patience when he said, "There is no gift that is better and more comprehensive than patience" (Bukhârî). Hence, patience as not only a virtue but a profound blessing, encompassing the strength and resilience needed to navigate life's challenges while remaining connected to Allāh.

Patience is also emphasised in the context of resisting temptations, as it requires exerting energy to refrain from sinful actions that one may be inclined to pursue. Ibn Qayyim (2009) explains that when a person's patience overpowers their whims and desires, they are akin to angels, who are free from such impulses. Conversely, when their desires for food, drink, and sexual gratification dominate their patience, they become like animals, driven purely by their base instincts while neglecting their intellectual and spiritual needs (Ibn Qayyim, 2009). Therefore, patience is closely tied to self-discipline, enabling one to resist temptations and avoid actions that are harmful.

The need for patience is especially significant when one is enduring hardships in life. Patience serves as a vital tool for overcoming life's greatest challenges. In moments when despair and hopelessness threaten to take hold, patience allows one to reframe difficulties in a more positive light. To prepare a Muslim for life's inevitable trials, the Qur'ân consistently reminds the believer that they will face tests, and when those tests arise, patience should be their guiding response. Through patience, believers are equipped to navigate adversity with resilience and faith, transforming hardship into an opportunity for growth and spiritual elevation. The reality of life being filled with tests is clearly mentioned in the Qur'ân:

ولنبْلُونَّكُم بِشىْ ء من ٱلْخوْفِ و ٱلْجُوع ونقْص من ٱلْأ مْولِ و ٱلْأ نفُسِ و ٱلثَّمرتِ وبشر
ٱلصَّبِرِين
ٱلَّذِين إِذا أصبتْهُم مُّصِيب قالُوٓ ا إِنَّا للِّ وإِنَّا إِليْهِ رجِعُو ن
أُولَٰئِك عليْهِم صلو ت من رَّبِهِمْ ورحْمة وأُولَٰئِك هُم ٱلْمُهْتدُو ن

- *We will certainly test you with something of fear and hunger, and loss of wealth and lives and fruits (earnings); but give glad tidings to the persevering and patient. Those who, when a disaster befalls them, say, "Surely we belong to God, and surely to Him we are bound to return." Such are those upon whom are blessings from their Lord and mercy and they are the rightly guided ones.*

(Al-Baqarah, 2:155–157, interpretation of the meaning)

Thus, tests and hardships in life are inevitable. When difficulties arise, Allāh counsels individuals to be patient, reminding them that He will account for all that they endure and will abundantly reward those who remain patient. Patience, therefore, requires a specific worldview, one that gives meaning to hardships in a way that offers peace to the heart and mind. This perspective involves acknowledging that there is Divine wisdom behind tests, and that great rewards await those who endure with patience.

Patience is closely linked to spiritual growth, as hardships act as a form of spiritual purification. Prophet Muḥammad ﷺ said, "Trials will not cease afflicting the believing man and the believing woman in their self, children, and wealth, until they meet Allāh without having any sin" (Tirmidhî). This understanding of the good that can emerge from hardships makes patience easier to practice, transforming difficulties into opportunities for spiritual elevation and allowing one to find contentment by viewing hardships in a new light.

If patience is one side of the coin, gratitude is considered the flipside of that coin as they are often seen as complementary. Prophet Muḥammad ﷺ said, "One who eats gratefully has the status of one who fasts patiently" (Ibn Mājah). As a projection of this *ḥadīth*, if patience is needed during hard times, gratitude is needed during good times.

Mental Health Benefits of **Ṣabr** *(Patience)*

Patience has substantial mental health benefits, particularly in building resilience, emotional regulation, achieving goals and overall mental well-being. Patience helps individuals manage stress more effectively by promoting self-control and the ability to navigate difficult circumstances by better managing impulses (Baumeister et al., 2007).

Studies suggest that patience prevents individuals from being overwhelmed by negative emotions, such as anger or frustration (Schnitker, 2012). As *ṣabr* involves trusting in a higher purpose or positive outcome, it encourages a hopeful outlook, reducing stress and anxiety during challenges. This makes patience a key factor in psychological resilience, enabling individuals to cope with life's uncertainties while maintaining mental stability.

Furthermore, patience contributes to long-term psychological well-being by nurturing contentment and life satisfaction. Patience leads to "well-being through increased goal achievement" (Schnitker, 2012, p. 278) due to patient people pursuing goals with more effort than less patient people, which means greater life achievements. Research also shows that those who practice patience experience fewer instances of impulsive, stress-inducing behaviours and instead adopt a mindset of acceptance and gratitude (Schnitker, 2012). This mindset helps individuals manage emotional distress more effectively and builds a sense of control over their reactions to external stressors. In viewing trials as opportunities for personal and spiritual growth, patience encourages a meaningful engagement with adversity, leading to greater happiness and a more profound sense of fulfilment in life.

Shukr (Gratitude)

Shukr stems from the triliteral root shīn kāf rā (ش ك ر). This root word occurs in 35 Chapters and appears 75 times in the Qur'ân, in five derived forms. *Shukr* literally means gladness felt about and gratitude shown for the good done to one. It is a term often encountered in the Qur'ân where the blessings of God are mentioned and how one should be grateful for them. Gratitude is strongly associated with strong faith and a connection with Allāh:

فَٱذْكُرُونِىٓ أَذْكُرْكُمْ وَٱشْكُرُوا۟ لِى وَلَا تَكْفُرُونِ

- *Then remember me and I will remember you. Be grateful to Me and do not reject me.*

(Al-Baqarah, 2:152,
interpretation of the meaning)

The importance of gratitude is further underlined when Allāh states that gratitude is the purpose of creation:

إلَيْهِ أخْرجكُم من بُطُون أُمَّهٰتِكُم لأ تعْلمُون شيًّا و جعل لكُم أُسَّمْع و آلْأ بْصٰر
وآلْأ فْد ة لعلَّكُم تشْكُرُو نَ

- *And Allāh brought you out of the wombs of your mothers while you knew nothing, and gave you hearing, sight, and intellect so perhaps you would be thankful.*

(An-Naḥl, 16:78,
interpretation of the meaning)

As with this verse, numerous times, the Qur'ān mentions the various blessings bestowed by Allāh on his creation. This acts as a reminder that humankind is immersed in numerous blessings. Blessings are often associated with material wealth or tangible goods, but they encompass much more than mere possessions. Ibn Qayyim illustrates this point through a story about Prophet Dawud's conversation with Allāh. Dawud asks, "What is the least of Your blessings?" In response, Allāh instructs him to take a breath and then says, "This is the least of My blessings upon you" (Ibn Qayyim, 2009, p. 19). Blessings further extend into the realm of human relationships, where the presence of supportive family, friends, and companions is a cherished part of life.

Most significantly, there are spiritual blessings, such as belief in Allāh, knowledge of Allāh, and love for Allāh. These spiritual blessings provide guidance, inner peace, and a deep sense of purpose, enriching one's life not only in this world but also with lasting benefits in the afterlife. Humankind is constantly being showered with blessings but one needs to have the eye to see it and the heart to feel it. Such an understanding of blessings calls for a state of constant gratitude, persisting until one's final breath.

وَإِذْ تَأَذَّنَ رَبُّكُمْ لَئِن شَكَرْتُمْ لَأَزِيدَنَّكُمْ

- *And remember when your Lord proclaimed, "If you are grateful, I will most certainly increase you"...*

(Ibrāhīm, 14:7,
interpretation of the meaning)

This promise from Allāh is an important declaration that highlights the transformative power of gratitude in a believer's life. This verse serves as a Divine principle that links human behaviour to Divine reward: the more one acknowledges and appreciates the blessings they have, the more Allāh will bestow upon them. Such a promise encourages the habitual practice of thankfulness, ultimately embedding gratitude into the individual's moral and psychological disposition, shaping it as a fundamental aspect of their character.

Over time, it becomes second nature to acknowledge and appreciate all forms of blessings. Prophet Muḥammad ﷺ emphasised this in the hādīth, "Whoever does not thank people, has not thanked Allāh Almighty" (Abī Dāwūd). Genuine gratitude involves appreciating all blessings, regardless of their size or source. Ultimately, gratitude is a mindset that involves recognising and expressing thanks for all the good in one's life, which fosters humility and contentment.

The interplay between patience and gratitude deepens when the different dimensions of gratitude are explored. At its most basic level, gratitude is expressed when one receives tangible blessings such as wealth, health, or success. However, as one advances in their spiritual journey, gratitude transcends this simple reciprocity and evolves into a deeper state. In this higher state, gratitude is not limited to what is visibly received but extends to what is withheld or delayed (Emmons & Crumpler, 2000). This advanced form of gratitude stems from a deep conviction that certain things may be withheld or delayed, by Allāh, because they are not ultimately beneficial, even if they appear so from a limited human perspective.

This understanding transforms the concept of blessings. What might initially be perceived as a setback, loss, or denial of a wish could, in fact, be a blessing in disguise. Allāh may be withholding what we perceive to be a blessing to prevents harm or to facilitate spiritual growth. This shift in perception aligns with the Qur'ânic wisdom:

وعسىٰ أن تكرهوا شيئًا وهو خيرٌ لكم وعسىٰ أن تحبوا شيئًا وهو شرٌ لكم والله
يعلم وأنتم لا تعلمو ن

- *Perhaps you dislike something which is good for you and like something which is bad for you. God knows and you do not know.*

(Al-Baqarah, 2:216, interpretation of the meaning)

This verse encapsulates the essence of deeper gratitude, where one trusts in Allāh's wisdom, recognising that true blessings are not always immediately visible or comprehensible. Sometimes what appears to be good, may actually be bad, and vice versa. On many occasions, the wisdom of situations manifests themselves over time, but sometimes one will need to wait for the afterlife to truly understand the wisdom of certain events, and this requires patience.

Thus, patience and gratitude are intertwined in these higher states of spirituality. Patience allows a person to endure what is withheld or delayed, while gratitude transforms that endurance into a recognition of unseen blessings. This holistic perspective on blessings encourages believers to maintain a state of thankfulness, whether their desires are fulfilled or not, ultimately strengthening their faith and reliance on Divine wisdom.

Mental Health Benefits of Shukr

In the last two decades, a "very large body of evidence has emerged suggesting that gratitude is strongly related to all aspects of well-being, on the basis of which promising clinical interventions have been developed" (Wood et al., 2010, p. 890). Research indicates that gratitude practices are associated with reduced levels of depression and anxiety, as they shift attention away from negative emotions and focus on the blessings one has (Emmons & McCullough, 2003). Gratitude has also been linked to higher levels of life satisfaction and optimism, both of which are crucial for maintaining emotional resilience in the face of adversity (Mccullough et al., 2004). By acknowledging and appreciating what one has, gratitude helps cultivate a positive mindset that improves emotional regulation and overall mental health.

Moreover, gratitude strengthens social bonds, which are essential for psychological well-being. "Gratitude is a moral affect that motivates prosocial behavior" (Emmons & McCullough, 2003, p. 387) such as kindness and empathy, leading to stronger interpersonal relationships (Algoe et al., 2010). These positive social interactions provide emotional support, which is vital in managing stress and maintaining a sense of belonging.

Furthermore, gratitude increases positive life orientation and psychological resilience by promoting a mindset of abundance rather than scarcity (Wood et al., 2010), reducing feelings of envy or frustration. Through fostering positive emotions and enhancing social connectedness, gratitude plays a critical role in promoting mental health and well-being.

Istiqāmah (Steadfastness)

فَاسْتَقِمْ كَمَا أُمِرْتَ

- *So, (O Muḥammad), remain steadfast in following the right way.*

(Hūd, 11:112,
interpretation of the meaning)

Istiqāmah stems from triliteral root qāf wāw mīm (م و ق). This root word occurs in 79 Chapters and appears 660 times in the Qur'ân, in 12 derived forms. *Istiqāmah* can be understood as stability, balance, constancy, and steadiness. In Islāmic terminology, it refers to leading a life that aligns with religious injunctions and morals as set forth by Allāh and exemplified by the Sunnah of the Prophet ﷺ, without veering into extremes. *Istiqāmah* is to remain steadfast and firm in one's faith and practice, adhering to the rules of the Qur'ân. Such firmness in faith, "encompasses all noble virtues, high moral standards, and good deeds" (Adamec, 2016, p. 222).

Allāh instructs in the Qur'ân:

فَٱسْتَقِمْ كَمَآ أُمِرْتَ وَمَن تَابَ مَعَكَ وَلَا تَطْغَوْا۟ ۚ إِنَّهُۥ بِمَا تَعْمَلُونَ بَصِيرٌ

- So, (O Muḥammad), remain steadfast in following the right way and let those who have returned with you (to the fold of faith and obedience) follow the right way as you were commanded, and do not exceed the proper limits of (devotion to Allāh). For certainly He is aware of all that you do.

(Hūd, 11:112,
interpretation of the meaning)

In relation to this verse, Ibn Abbas noted, "No verse revealed to the Prophet was more burdensome or of greater concern to him than this verse." When the Prophet's Companions remarked, "Your hair has started to turn grey," he responded, "Chapter Hud and its sisters have turned my hair grey" (Tirmidhî), specifically referring to the verse "Therefore remain steadfast..." (Ma'arif al-Qur'ân, 11:112). This highlights how seriously the Prophet took this command to remain steadfast in the face of challenges. Moreover, it underscores the significant ongoing effort required to maintain steadfastness in devotion and adherence to Allāh's commands.

Istiqāmah means being alert to possible deviation at the beginning, engaging in self-supervision during the journey, being closed to wrong thoughts and actions, and considering only Allāh's pleasure and approval at the end. These are significant elements to maintain a state of *istiqāmah*. There is an ongoing consistency in intentions rather than wavering at some point in one's journey. Thus, starting with the correct mindset and heartset does not guarantee the same ending. One must have *istiqāmah* throughout the process to ensure there is no deviation at the beginning, the middle, nor at the end.

There is immense reward promised by Allāh for those who maintain *istiqāmah* in one's faith and actions. The greatest of these rewards is Paradise, as described in the Qur'ân:

إن الَّذِينقالُوا ربُّنا إليْهِ ثُم استَقمُوا تتنزَّل عليْهم الْملٰئِكة الَّاتخافُوا ولَا تحْزنُوا
وأ بْشِرُوا بِ اَلْجنَّةِ اَلَّتِى كُنتُم تُو عدُو ن

- *Verily, those who say, "Our Lord is Allāh" and then they remain firm and straight, on them the Angels will descend (at the time of death), saying: "Fear not, nor grieve! But receive glad tidings of Paradise which you have been promised!"*

(Fuṣṣilat, 41:30,
interpretation of the meaning)

This verse illustrates the immense spiritual reward awaiting those who remain unwavering in their belief and righteousness. As they approach the moment of death, angels descend to console and reassure them, removing all fear and sorrow. They are given the ultimate glad tidings of entry into Paradise, a reward that reflects the magnitude of maintaining steadfastness in faith. This Divine promise not only highlights the importance of *istiqāmah* but also the mercy and generosity of Allāh, who assures His steadfast servants of eternal bliss for their perseverance and dedication.

As a final point, Abu 'Amr's question to the Prophet is worth noting, "I said: 'O Messenger of Allāh, tell me something about Islām which I could not ask anyone about save you.' The Prophet ﷺ answered: 'Say: I believe in Allāh, and then stand firm and steadfast'" (Muslim). Out of all possible advice the Prophet could have given, he emphasised *istiqāmah*, steadfastness. This choice underscores the fundamental importance of *istiqāmah* in Islām. It highlights that belief in Allāh is the foundation, but the true test lies in consistently upholding that belief with unwavering dedication, no matter the challenges. The Prophet's advice reflects how *istiqāmah* is essential for success in this life and the Hereafter, as it sustains a believer's connection to Allāh through faith, action, and perseverance.

Mental Health Benefits of Istiqāmah

Istiqāmah provides significant mental health benefits by promoting resilience in the face of life's challenges. The practice of *istiqāmah* encourages individuals to maintain a consistent commitment to their Islāmic faith, even during difficult times. This steadfastness creates a strong sense of purpose and direction. In the Islāmic context, *istiqāmah* involves staying true to one's devotion to Allāh and moral principles, which fosters a sense of inner peace and mental clarity by aligning actions with spiritual values.

Additionally, *istiqāmah* enhances self-discipline and perseverance, leading to self-control which "refers to the capacity for altering one's own responses, especially to bring them into line with standards such as ideals, values, morals, and social expectations, and to support the pursuit of long-term goals" (Baumeister et al., 2007, p. 351). This is a key quality in building emotional resilience. By maintaining consistency in righteous actions, individuals develop a mindset of patience and endurance. Research on self-discipline and goal persistence highlights the positive impact of long-term commitment on psychological well-being, as it nurtures self-efficacy and reduces feelings of helplessness (Baumeister et al., 2007). In this way, *istiqāmah* serves as a powerful tool for mental health, fostering mental strength, spiritual alignment, and resilience against life's uncertainties.

Conclusion

The Qur'ânic concepts, *ṣabr* (patience), *shukr* (gratitude), and *istiqāmah* (steadfastness) are essential for both spiritual and psychological well-being. *Ṣabr* teaches resilience and endurance during life's challenges, allowing individuals to remain calm and hopeful. *Shukr* fosters a positive outlook by encouraging gratitude for blessings, which enhances emotional stability and overall contentment with life. *Istiqāmah* offers consistent alignment between faith and actions, and stability, promoting a sense of purpose and inner peace. By integrating these concepts into daily life, individuals can navigate life's trials with strength, contentment, and a steadfast commitment to their spiritual journey, while maintaining their mental well-being.

References

Abī Dāwūd. In-book reference: Book 43, Hadith 39. English translation: Book 42, Hadith 4793. https://sunnah.com/abudawud:4811.

Adamec, L. W. (2016). *Historical dictionary of Islam*. Rowman & Littlefield.

Algoe, S. B., Gable, S. L., & Maisel, N. C. (2010). It's the little things: Everyday gratitude as a booster shot for romantic relationships. *Personal Relationships*, *17*(2), 217–233.

Baumeister, R. F., Vohs, K. D., & Tice, D. M. (2007). The strength model of self-control. *Current Directions in Psychological Science*, *16*(6), 351–355.

Bukhârî. In-book reference: Book 81, Hadith 59. English translation: Vol. 8, Book 76, Hadith 477. https://sunnah.com/bukhari:6470.

Emmons, R. A., & Crumpler, C. A. (2000). Gratitude as a human strength: Appraising the evidence. *Journal of Social and Clinical Psychology, 19*(1), 56–69. https://doi.org/10.1521/jscp.2000.19.1.56.

Emmons, R. A., & McCullough, M. E. (2003). Counting blessings versus burdens: An experimental investigation of gratitude and subjective well-being in daily life. *Journal of Personality and social Psychology*, *84*(2), 377–389.

Esposito, J. L. (2004). *The Oxford dictionary of Islam*. Oxford University Press.

Ibn Mājah. In-book reference: Book 7, Hadith 128. English translation: Vol. 1, Book 7, Hadith 1765. https://sunnah.com/ibnmajah:1765.

Ibn Qayyim. (2009). *Patience and gratitude*. Ta-Ha Publishers Ltd.

Ma'arif Al-Qur'ân. (n.d.). *Quran.com*. Retrieved from https://quran.com/en/11:112/tafsirs/en-tafsir-maarif-ul-quran (accessed 9 September 2024).

McCullough, M. E., Tsang, J. A., & Emmons, R. A. (2004). Gratitude in intermediate affective terrain: Links of grateful moods to individual differences and daily emotional experience. *Journal of Personality and Social Psychology*, *86*(2), 295–309.

Muslim. In-book reference: Book 1, Hadith 66. English translation: Book 1, Hadith 62. https://sunnah.com/muslim/1/66.

Schnitker, S. A. (2012). An examination of patience and well-being. *The Journal of Positive Psychology*, *7*(4), 263–280.

Tirmidhî. In-book reference: Book 36, Hadith 97. English translation: Vol. 4, Book 10, Hadith 2399. https://sunnah.com/tirmidhi:2399.

Wood, A. M., Froh, J. J., & Geraghty, A. W. (2010). Gratitude and well-being: A review and theoretical integration. *Clinical Psychology Review*, *30*(7), 890–905.

8 Qur'ânic Spiritual Concepts of *Tawbah*, *Istighfār*, *Riḍā*, *Sakīna*, and *Iṭmīnān*

Introduction

This chapter continues the discussion of Qur'ânic spiritual concepts that serve as valuable tools for navigating life, offering guidance and direction for everyday life experiences. *Tawbah* (repentance) encourages sincere repentance and turning back to Allah after sin, while *istighfār* (asking for forgiveness) is an essential component of tawbah that is an important aspect of spiritual cleansing and overall success. *Riḍā* teaches contentment with Allah's will, helping to reduce dissatisfaction. *Sakīna* brings tranquillity during hardship, and *iṭmīnān* represents the ultimate state of peace and trust in Allah's plan. These concepts provide spiritual guidance for navigating life's challenges while promoting mental well-being.

Tawbah (Repentance)

Tawbah stems from the triliteral root tā wāw bā (ت و ب). This root word occurs in 25 Chapters and appears 87 times in the Qur'ân, in four derived forms. Linguistically, the word *tawbah* is a noun meaning "to return." Specifically, to return from one state to another. In the context of repentance, *tawbah* signifies returning from rebellion and sin to the straight path of virtue. It involves turning away from major sins and embracing sincere repentance. Thus, *tawbah* is characterised by deep regret and remorse for past wrongdoings, accompanied by a commitment to turn back to Allāh with the intention of obeying Him moving forward.

Tawbah is usually used with *naṣūḥ*, literally meaning pure, sincere, reforming, improving, and repairing. *Tawbah naṣūḥ* means a pure, sincere repentance that perfectly reforms and improves the one who feels it. It implies a genuine repentance where there is heartfelt remorse for the wrong committed

DOI: 10.4324/9781003494614-8

and great effort made to right the wrong. One example where *tawbah naṣūḥ* is mentioned in the Qur'ân is as follows:

يَٰٓأَيُّهَا ا لَّذِين ءَامَنُوا أَيُّهَا تُوبُوٓا إِلَى ٱللَّ تَوْبَةً نَّصُو حا عَسَ ى رَبُّكُمْ أَن يُكَفِرَ عَنكُمْ سَيِّاتِكُم
وَيُدْخِلَكُمْ جَنَّت تَجْرِى مِن تَحْتِهَا ٱلْنَّهَرُ ُ

- *Oh, you who believe! Turn to Allāh in true, sincere repentance: in the hope that your Lord will remove from you your evil deeds and admit you to Gardens beneath which rivers flow.*

(At-Taḥrīm, 66:8,
interpretation of the meaning)

Allāh's love for those who repent is also clearly emphasised:

إِنَّ ٱللَّهَ يُحِبُّ ٱلتَّوَّٰبِينَ وَيُحِبُّ ٱلْمُتَطَهِّرِينَ

- *Surely Allāh loves those who turn to Him in sincere repentance, and He loves those who cleanse themselves.*

(Al-Baqarah, 2:222,
interpretation of the meaning)

This verse highlights a central tenet of Islāmic spirituality; the immense mercy and forgiveness of Allāh, which is always available to those who seek it with sincerity. Repentance, or *tawbah*, is not just an act of seeking forgiveness; it is a sign of humility and recognition of one's shortcomings before Allāh. When a believer turns to Allāh in repentance, they are acknowledging His sovereignty and mercy, and their willingness to return to the path of righteousness.

Furthermore, the call to repentance acknowledges human imperfection. Every human being is prone to making mistakes and sinning, but Allāh, in His infinite mercy, provides the path of repentance as a means of returning to Him. In this act of repentance, a believer demonstrates humility, acknowledging their shortcomings and their need for Allāh's forgiveness.

Allāh loves those who turn to Him in repentance, which shows His willingness to forgive and accept those who sincerely seek His mercy. This is reinforced in various verses:

وَمَن يَعْمَلْ سُوٓءًا أَوْ يَظْلِمْ نَفْسَهُۥ ثُمَّ يَسْتَغْفِرِ ٱللَّهَ يَجِدِ ٱللَّهَ غَفُورًا رَّحِيمًا

- *And whoever does a wrong or wrongs himself but then seeks forgiveness of Allāh will find Allāh Forgiving and Merciful.*

(An-Nisā', 4:110,
interpretation of the meaning)

قُل لِّذِينَآيَ علَّذِين أَسْرَفُوا أَنفُسِهِم عَلَى أَنفُسِهِمواتَقْنَطُوا مِن رَّحْمَةِ ٱللَّ إِن ٱللَّ يَغْفِرُ ٱلذُّنُو ب جَمِيعا إِنَّهُ هُ و ٱلْغَفُورُ ٱلرَّحِيمُ

- *Say, "Oh My servants who have transgressed against themselves [by sinning], do not despair of the mercy of Allāh. Indeed, Allāh forgives all sins. Indeed, it is He who is the Forgiving, the Merciful".*

(Az-Zumar, 39:53,
the interpretation of the meaning)

The word used in the verse, *tawwābīn*, denotes those who repent continuously. This suggests that repentance is not a one-time act but a continuous process. It reflects the believer's ongoing struggle to stay on the righteous path and their constant return to Allāh after every fall. A believer is reminded to regularly engage in self-reflection, repentance, and purification, knowing that these actions bring them closer to Allāh and earn His love.

It is human nature to commit sins, and this is acknowledged in the words of Prophet Muḥammad ﷺ; "If you were not to commit sins, Allāh would sweep you out of existence and would replace you by other people who would commit sins, and then would ask forgiveness from Allāh" (Muslim (a)). Committing sins is part of what it means to be human, but what is important is to ask Allāh for forgiveness when one does commit sins, since "All human beings are sinners; the best of the sinners are those who repent" (Tirmidhî (a)).

A key aspect of *tawbah* is to not lose hope in Allāh's mercy, nor to limit His mercy; "Verily Allāh the Almighty will accept the repentance of his servants right until the last moments of his death" (Tirmidhî (b)). Repentance is such a powerful act that, "The one who repents from a sin is like the one who has no sin" (Ibn Mājah).

Tawbah does have its conditions:

1 One refrains from committing the same sin again.
2 There is a feeling guilt for the sin that was committed.
3 A firm intention is made to not commit that sin again.

While some individuals may be able to meet all the criteria for repentance, others may struggle, particularly if they lack confidence in their ability to cease the sin, as is often the case with addictions. In such situations, making *du'ā'* to Allāh for help in overcoming the grip of the sin is a crucial step in the right direction. It is important to remember that *tawbah* should not be withheld simply because one fears they may fall into the sin again. The Prophet Muḥammad ﷺ said, "By Allāh, I seek forgiveness from Allāh and turn to Him in repentance more than seventy times a day" (Bukhârî). Through this *ḥadīth*, the Prophet (pbuh) teaches believers that repentance is not a one-time event.

Rather, seeking forgiveness and turning back to Allāh should be a continual practice, woven into the fabric of daily life.

The following hādīth beautifully captures the way Allāh receives those who repent, providing a great incentive for all believers to repent, for there is nothing more a believer wants than for Allāh to be pleased with them:

Allāh's Messenger ﷺ said:

> Allāh is more pleased with the repentance of His believing servant than a person who loses his riding beast carrying food and drink. He sleeps (being disappointed of its recovery) and then gets up and goes in search for that, until he is stricken with thirst. Then comes back to the place where he had been before and goes to sleep completely exhausted placing his head upon his hands waiting for death. And when he gets up, there is before him his riding beast and his provisions of food and drink. Allāh is more pleased with the repentance of His servant than the recovery of this riding beast along with the provisions (of food and drink.
>
> (Muslim (b))

There are so many benefits and incentives provided by Allāh for believers to repent; He replaces their evil deeds with good deeds (Al-Furqān, 25:70), the repentant earn the praises of the angels (Ghāfir, 40:7), Allāh promises them paradise (Āl ʿImrān, 3:135–136), it is a means of happiness in this life (Hūd, 11:3), and there is no limit to the number of sins that Allāh forgives (Az-Zumar, 39:53).

Through numerous Qur'ânic verses, Allāh consistently provides a wealth of incentives and reassurances, emphasising His readiness to forgive those who sincerely repent. He extends His mercy, offering believers the hope of not only absolution but also immense rewards for their sincere efforts to return to Him. These Divine promises serve as a powerful encouragement, reminding believers that no matter how far they may have strayed, Allāh's door of mercy remains open. By assuring them of His forgiveness, Allāh motivates believers to continuously seek His pardon, reinforcing the idea that repentance is always met with Divine compassion and a chance for renewal, both spiritually and in the pursuit of righteousness.

Mental Health Benefits of* Tawbah *(Repentance)

Tawbah enhances emotional resilience by encouraging personal growth and self-improvement. Repentance involves not only asking for forgiveness but also committing to change, which nurtures a mindset of growth and renewal due to its action-oriented nature. This process requires self-awareness and emotional regulation, key factors in maintaining psychological well-being (Worthington & Wade, 2020). By promoting a sense of accountability and the possibility of redemption, *tawbah* allows individuals to let go of past mistakes and action positive personal development. This shift in perspective can reduce depressive symptoms and increase life satisfaction through empowerment, as individuals learn to transform their past experiences into opportunities for growth and learning.

From a more nuanced perspective, Rothman explains that "Tawbah is not about beating ourselves up over our mistakes, nor is it about dwelling in feelings of guilt" (Rothman, 2018, p. 39). Keeping in mind that *tawbah* means to return, "It's about recognizing our reliance on God and recentering our focus on the greater reality of our existence over the distractions within our nafs (self) and the dunya" (Rothman, 2018, p. 39). This alignment and (re)connection with Allāh can have an immense positive impact on one's spiritual heart and hence one's spiritual and mental well-being.

Istighfār (Asking for Forgiveness)

أَسْتَغْفِرُوا رَبَّكُمْ إِنَّهُ كَانَ غَفَّارًا

- *Ask forgiveness of your Lord. Indeed, He is ever a Perpetual Forgiver.*

(Nūḥ, 71:10,
interpretation of the meaning)

Istighfār stems from the triliteral root ghayn fā rā (غ ف ر). This root word occurs in 56 Chapters and appears 234 times in the Qur'ân, in seven derived forms. *Istighfār* (seeking forgiveness from Allāh) is a crucial element of *tawbah* (repentance). While *tawbah* refers to the act of returning from sin to the path of righteousness, *istighfār* is the verbal expression of asking Allāh for forgiveness for those sins. It is represented in heartfelt phrases uttered like *astaghfirullah*, meaning "I ask You for Your forgiveness," spoken with remorse for one's actions. In contrast, *tawbah* encompasses the broader process of repentance, which involves feeling regret for the sin, ceasing the wrongful behaviour, and committing to avoid it in the future. Thus, *istighfār* is a key component of *tawbah*, as it expresses the remorse that underpins true repentance. Both are essential, since *tawbah* would be incomplete without *istighfār*.

The Qur'ân frequently emphasises the importance of *istighfār*, portraying it as a means of spiritual cleansing, Divine mercy, and personal growth. Allāh commands the believers to seek His forgiveness, assuring them of His mercy and readiness to forgive those who turn to Him sincerely:

ذَا لَّذِين ٱ و أَو فَ حِشَة فَعَلُواأَنفُسَهُم ظَلَمُوٓاٱ ف للَّ ٱ ذَكَرُواستَغْفَرُوا لِذُنُوبِهِمْ وَمَن يَغْفِرُ
لَمللَّ ٱإِلَّ لذُّنُوب ٱ مَا عَلَى يُصِرُّوا فَعَلُوا وَهُ م يَعْلَمُو ن

- *And those who, when they commit an immorality or wrong themselves (by transgression), remember Allāh and seek forgiveness for their sins—and who can forgive sins except Allāh? And (who) do not persist in what they have done while they know.*

(Āl ʿImrān, 3:135, interpretation of the meaning)

Not only does Allāh assure believers that seeking forgiveness opens the doors to His mercy and blessings, but He also expresses His readiness to forgive:

قُل يَعِبَادِى قُلل أنفسِهِم عَلَى أَسْرَفُوا تَقْنَطُوا مِن رَّحْمَةِ ٱللَّ إِ ن ٱللَّ يَغْفِرُ ٱلذُّنُو ب
جَمِيعاا إِنَّه ہُ و ٱلْغَفُورُ ٱلرَّحِيمُ

- *Say, "Oh My servants who have transgressed against themselves [by sinning], do not despair of the mercy of Allāh. Indeed, Allāh forgives all sins. Indeed, it is He who is the Forgiving, the Merciful".*

(Az-Zumar, 39:53,
interpretation of the meaning)

Beyond spiritual cleansing, the Qur'ân connects *istighfār* with various worldly and spiritual blessings. It is portrayed as a means to attain peace, prosperity, and success. In Chapter Nuh, for example, Prophet Nuh (Noah) advises his people to seek forgiveness from Allāh, promising them both material and spiritual rewards:

فَقُلْتُ ٱسْتَغْفِرُوا رَبَّكُمْ إِنَّهُۥ كَانَ غَفَّارًا
يُرْسِلِ ٱلسَّمَآءَ عَلَيْكُم مِّدْرَارًا
وَيُمْدِدْكُم بِأَمْوَٰلٍ وَبَنِينَ وَيَجْعَل لَّكُمْ جَنَّـٰتٍ وَيَجْعَل لَّكُمْ أَنْهَـٰرًا

- *And said, "Ask forgiveness of your Lord. Indeed, He is ever a Perpetual Forgiver. He will send [rain from] the sky upon you in [continuing] showers and give you increase in wealth and children and provide for you gardens and provide for you, rivers".*

(Nūḥ, 71:10–12,
interpretation of the meaning)

Prophet Muḥammad ﷺ also highlights the multiple worldly benefits of *istighfār*;

"If anyone constantly seeks pardon (from Allāh), Allāh will appoint for him a way out of every distress and a relief from every anxiety and will provide sustenance for him from where he expects not" (Abī Dāwūd).

Prophet Muḥammad ﷺ not only emphasises the spiritual benefits of seeking forgiveness but also underscores the practical and worldly advantages. In the above-mentioned *ḥadīth*, the Prophet conveys the message that regular practice of *istighfār* leads to numerous beneficial outcomes in a believer's life. By persistently turning to Allāh and seeking His pardon, one can experience tangible relief from life's difficulties.

The phrase "Allāh will appoint for him a way out of every distress" suggests that when someone consistently asks for forgiveness, they are granted Divine assistance in navigating their challenges. Life is filled with various hardships, whether they are emotional, financial, or related to personal relationships.

Istighfār becomes a source of relief, easing burdens that may feel insurmountable. The relief from every anxiety mentioned here signifies that Allāh's mercy extends to providing inner peace by helping a person manage stress, fear, and worry.

Moreover, the *ḥadīth* promises unexpected sustenance: "and will provide sustenance for him from where he expects not." This indicates that Allāh provides not just spiritual rewards but also material provisions. It reassures believers that the act of sincerely seeking forgiveness invites blessings and opportunities beyond what they could have foreseen or planned. In essence, the worldly benefits of *istighfār* are interconnected with the spiritual act of turning back to Allāh, serving as a reminder of Allāh's boundless mercy.

Istighfār is also portrayed as a means of protection from Divine punishment. The Qur'ân indicates that Allāh would not punish a people as long as they engage in seeking forgiveness:

وَمَا كَانَ ٱللَّهُ لِيُعَذِّبَهُمْ وَأَنتَ فِيهِمْ ۚ وَمَا كَانَ ٱللَّهُ مُعَذِّبَهُمْ وَهُمْ يَسْتَغْفِرُونَ

- *But Allāh would not punish them while you, [O Muḥammad], are among them, and Allāh would not punish them while they seek forgiveness.*

(Al-Anfāl, 8:33,
interpretation of the meaning)

Seeking forgiveness is recommended as part of a believer's daily routine, ensuring that hearts remain pure and relationships with Allāh are kept strong:

قَوْلَهُم كَان وَمَا قَالُوا رَبَّنَا ٱغْفِرْ لَنَا ذُنُوبَنَا وَإِسْرَافَنَا فِيٓ أَمْرِنَا وَثَبِّ تْ أَقْدَامَنَا
وَ ٱنصُرْنَا عَلَى ٱلْقَوْمِ ٱلْكَ فِرِينَ

- *And [those] who say, "Our Lord, forgive us our sins and the excess [committed] in our affairs and plant firmly our feet and give us victory over the disbelieving people".*

(Āl ʿImrān, 3:147,
interpretation of the meaning)

Istighfār is a powerful act of worship that permeates the teachings of the Qur'ân. It is a means of drawing closer to Allāh, attaining His mercy, and achieving both spiritual and worldly success. By regularly engaging in *istighfār*, believers purify their hearts, secure their Lord's forgiveness, and open the doors to countless blessings. The Qur'ân's emphasis on *istighfār* encourages Muslims to develop a continuous practice of seeking forgiveness, recognising it as an essential aspect of their relationship with Allāh, but also as a means to happiness in this life and the next.

Mental Health Benefits of Istighfār

Itighfar (repentance) offers mental health benefits by facilitating emotional healing and self-forgiveness. When individuals engage in seeking forgiveness, they often experience relief from feelings of guilt and shame, emotions that can weigh heavily on mental well-being (Tangney et al., 2007).

Research suggests that guilt, when unresolved, can lead to stress, anxiety, and depression (Bybee & Quiles, 1998). *Istighfār* allows individuals to confront their mistakes, seek forgiveness from Allāh, and move forward with the hope of having a clean slate. This process promotes inner peace by breaking the cycle of self-blame while fostering emotional release, leading to improved mental health outcomes. As individuals acknowledge their wrongdoings and seek redemption, they experience a sense of spiritual and emotional cleansing, which reduces feelings of spiritual, emotional, and psychological burden.

Riḍā (Contentment)

ٱرْجِعِىٓ إِلَىٰ رَبِّكِ رَاضِيَةً

- *Return to your Lord, well pleased (with Him)...*

(Al-Fajr, 89:28,
interpretation of the meaning)

Riḍā stems from the triliteral root rā ḍād wāw (ر ض و). This root word occurs in 32 Chapters and appears 73 times in the Qur'ân, in nine derived forms. *Riḍā*, often translated as contentment, can also be understood as resignation and satisfaction. In its essence, *riḍā* means to be free from any form of discontent, resentment, or rebellion against Allāh's will. It is a state where a believer is pleased with Allāh's decisions and is grateful for every situation, whether it brings joy or hardship. This contentment is not merely passive acceptance but an active engagement with life, where one trusts in Allāh's wisdom and mercy. That is, contentment is not just about accepting one's fate but also embracing it with a tranquil heart and mind.

Riḍā can be divided into two types: contentment with Allāh and contentment with what comes from Allāh. This refers to a believer's satisfaction with Allāh as their Lord. It involves being at peace with Allāh and the way He arranges one's life, including the trials and tribulations that one encounters. This type of contentment is rooted in a deep faith that Allāh's wisdom surpasses human understanding, and thus, whatever He decrees is ultimately for the best (Al-Qushayrī, 2007). The arrangement of affairs relates to accepting the specific circumstances and events that Allāh brings into one's life. Whether these events are perceived as positive or negative, a believer who practices *riḍā* sees all events as part of Allāh's Divine plan and accepts them without complaint. This acceptance is accompanied by a sense of peace and a belief that every occurrence has a purpose in the grand design of the universe.

Rabi'a al-Adawiyyah (d. 801) views contentment as transcending mere acceptance of Allāh's decree. She describes it as the ability to rejoice in afflictions as much as one rejoices in blessings (Al-Qushayrī, 2007), leading to a state where a person experiences the same elation regardless of whether they encounter good or bad, positive or negative circumstances. In this understanding of contentment, suffering evokes the same joyful reaction as a happy experience. Thus, contentment "is not about patiently enduring the challenges of life, but rather finding happiness in poverty and affliction" (Schimmel & Ernst, 2011, p. 126).

However, the idea of rejoicing in afflictions is challenging. As a result, contentment is understood to exist in levels, with an ordinary person's experience of contentment differing from that of someone with deep spirituality. For most people, it involves accepting what Allāh has willed without objection and willingly ordering one's life according to His commandments, in submission to His Lordship and Divine authority. For those with deeper spiritual knowledge, they experience contentment at a higher level, which means embracing Allāh's decrees and ordinances without objection. At this level, one's connection with Allāh is so constant that no experience causes the heart to waver. The highest level of contentment is attained by those with intense spirituality. At this stage, a person is aligned with what pleases Allāh, and emotions like anger, joy, or grief are no longer felt for personal reasons. Such an individual, having transcended personal feelings, thoughts, and desires, is able to focus on what Allāh wills. In this state, it is not about what the self wants; the driving force becomes what pleases Allāh and emotions are felt accordingly.

The following Qur'ānic verse encompasses these levels of contentment:

يَـٰٓأَيَّتُهَا ٱلنَّفْسُ ٱلْمُطْمَئِنَّةُ
ٱرْجِعِىٓ إِلَىٰ رَبِّكِ رَاضِيَةً مَّرْضِيَّةً
فَٱدْخُلِى فِى عِبَـٰدِى
وَٱدْخُلِى جَنَّتِى

- *Oh, you soul at peace (muṭma'innah). Return to your Lord, well-pleased (with Him) (raḍiyyah), and well-pleasing to Him (marḍiyyah). Enter, then, among My servants! And enter my Paradise!*

(Al-Fajr, 89:27–30, interpretation of the meaning)

Being content with Allāh's judgement and being unconditionally pleased with Him become a source of spiritual peace and happiness in both worlds. The contentment is reciprocated with Allāh being pleased with the person who is content. Such a positive reciprocal relationship becomes the foundation of serenity and peacefulness.

Mental Health Benefits of Contentment

When individuals practice *riḍā*, they develop an acceptance of life's circumstances and trust in Allāh's wisdom. Ultimately, *riḍā* is associated with contentment, satisfaction, and good pleasure based on the serene acceptance of *qadar* (Divine will) (Khalil, 2014). Contentment allows individuals to let go of the constant desire for more, replacing it with gratitude for what they already have, thus *riḍā* is strongly linked with *shukr* (gratitude).

Additionally, *riḍā* encourages emotional stability by reducing feelings of dissatisfaction and envy, which can otherwise lead to emotional turmoil. Contentment helps individuals focus on the blessings in their lives, decreasing negative emotions like frustration, regret, and envy. Studies in positive psychology emphasise that contentment is closely tied to higher life satisfaction and well-being (Sheldon & Lyubomirsky, 2007). In the Islāmic context, *riḍā* enhances mental health by fostering reliance on Allāh's plan and reducing the emotional disturbances caused by unmet desires. This acceptance helps create a sense of emotional freedom and inner tranquillity, promoting long-term psychological well-being.

Sakīna (Serenity)

هُوَ ٱلَّذِىٓ أَنزَلَ ٱلسَّكِينَةَ فِى قُلُوبِ ٱلْمُؤْمِنِينَ لِيَزْدَادُوٓا۟ إِيمَـٰنًا مَّعَ إِيمَـٰنِهِمْ

- *He is the One Who sent down serenity upon the hearts of the believers so that they may increase even more in their faith.*

(Al-Fatḥ, 48:4,
interpretation of the meaning)

Sakīna stems from the triliteral root sīn kāf nūn (ن ك س). This root word occurs in 40 Surahs and appears 69 times in the Qur'ân, in six derived forms. *Sakīna* literally means calmness, silence, and steadiness so that a person experiences tranquillity. In the context of Islāmic spirituality, it also means the heart has come to a rest as a result of its connection with Allāh so it is not shaken by worldly fear, grief, or anxiety, finding peace, integrity, and harmony between their inner world and the outer world.

Someone with serenity, therefore, can deal with the challenges and difficulties that come with life without being unsettled by such experiences. Serenity is affiliated with the unseen realm rather than drawing its strength from the world that the physical eye can see. For example, a substance that resembled vapour or mist is believed to have surrounded Usayd ibn Khudayr, one of the companions of Prophet Muḥammad ﷺ, while he was reading the Qur'ān, which gave him a feeling of exhilaration. This feeling of exhilaration is attributed to serenity. Thus, it is like a positive energy that surrounds a person, giving them a feeling of peace, an experience that cannot be fully explained through the physical world.

Serenity is mentioned in the Qur'ān as a means of reaffirming one's faith:

هُوَ ٱلَّذِىٓ أَنزَلَ ٱلسَّكِينَةَ فِى قُلُوبِ ٱلْمُؤْمِنِينَ لِيَزْدَادُوٓا۟ إِيمَـٰنًا مَّعَ إِيمَـٰنِهِمْ

- *He is the One Who sent down serenity upon the hearts of the believers so that they may increase even more in their faith ...*

(Al-Fatḥ, 48:4,
interpretation of the meaning)

Maḥallī and Suyūṭī (2007) describe serenity as a spirit of peace sent down by Allāh as a Divine reassurance to those who believe. Ibn 'Abbās (2008) explains how serenity further reaffirms and strengthens the faith of the believer, adding certainty, belief, and knowledge to the faith that one already has.

Mental Health Benefits of Sakīna

Sakīna (tranquillity) offers mental health benefits by cultivating a state of inner calm and emotional balance. In the Islāmic tradition, *sakīna* refers to a sense of peace granted by Allāh, often experienced during moments of deep faith and trust in Him. This tranquillity helps individuals manage anxiety and stress, providing emotional relief during times of hardship. Research in psychology indicates that feelings of calm and inner peace are associated with lower levels of cortisol, the hormone responsible for stress (Hölzel et al., 2011). By fostering a sense of connection to a higher power, *sakīna* alleviates the mental pressure of life's uncertainties, reducing worry and promoting a more stable emotional state.

Furthermore, *sakīna* enhances mental well-being by promoting mindfulness and present-centred awareness. In moments of tranquillity, individuals are better able to focus on the present, letting go of fears about the future or regrets about the past. This present-centred awareness aligns with the principles of mindfulness, which research has shown to reduce symptoms of anxiety and depression while improving overall well-being (Brown & Ryan, 2003). The spiritual dimension of *sakīna* deepens this sense of calm, as individuals trust in Allāh's guidance and feel protected in His care. This emotional stability and mindfulness foster resilience, allowing individuals to navigate challenges with a sense of peace and clarity.

Iṭmīnān (Peacefulness)

يَـٰٓأَيَّتُهَا ٱلنَّفْسُ ٱلْمُطْمَئِنَّةُ

- *Oh, soul at peace!*

(Al-Fajr, 89:27,
interpretation of the meaning)

Iṭmīnān stems from the triliteral root ṭā mīm nūn (ط م ن). This root word occurs in 11 Surahs and appears 13 times in the Qur'ân, in two derived forms. *Iṭmīnān* (peacefulness) is defined as full satisfaction and contentment so that one is in a state of complete rest. It is a state of a heart that is at peace, free from the disturbances of doubt, fear, or worry. *Iṭmīnān* represents the soul's stability, where it remains unshaken by the trials and tribulations of life.

Iṭmīnān is a spiritual state surpassing serenity; if serenity is understood to be the "beginning of being freed from theoretical knowledge and awakened to the truth, *iṭmīnān* (peacefulness) is considered to be the final point or station" (Ibn 'Abbās, 2008, p. 685). In other words, serenity eventually leads to peacefulness.

The Qur'ān mentions peacefulness as a level of the *nafs* (self) that one aspires to achieve:

يَـٰٓأَيَّتُهَا ٱلنَّفْسُ ٱلْمُطْمَئِنَّةُ
ٱرْجِعِىٓ إِلَىٰ رَبِّكِ رَاضِيَةً مَّرْضِيَّةً
فَٱدْخُلِى فِى عِبَـٰدِى
وَٱدْخُلِى جَنَّتِى

- *Oh, soul at peace! Return to your Lord, well-pleased (with Him), and well-pleasing to Him. Enter, then, among My servants (fully content with servanthood to Me)! And enter my Paradise!*

(Al-Fajr, 89:27–30,
interpretation of the meaning)

Based on this Qur'ānic verse, there is a connection between peacefulness and contentment: when *raḍiyyah* (being content with Allāh) and *marḍiyyah* (Allāh being content with you) is achieved, it means a person has reached a state of peacefulness. Therefore, peacefulness is the result of having contentment with Allāh and all that He has decreed, but it also necessitates reciprocation of contentment by Allāh.

Further, those who have acquired this rank find the greatest peace when they feel connected with Allāh. This notion has been expressed in the Qur'ān in the verse:

أَلَا بِذِكْرِ ٱللَّهِ تَطْمَئِنُّ ٱلْقُلُوبُ

- *Indeed, in the remembrance of Allāh do hearts find peace (tatma-innu).*

(Ar-Ra'd, 13:28,
interpretation of the meaning)

When a believer constantly remembers Allāh, their heart becomes tranquil, and they experience a profound sense of peace, regardless of external circumstances. This tranquillity is a sign of the heart's connection to Allāh, where it finds solace and comfort. *Iṭmīnān* is a crucial element in a believer's spiritual growth. As a person progresses in their faith, the tranquillity of their heart reflects the strength of their connection with Allāh. This inner peace enables the believer to navigate life's difficulties with patience, trust, and resilience. *Iṭmīnān* also fosters a deeper sense of gratitude and contentment, as the believer recognises that true peace comes from Allāh alone.

Mental Health Benefits of **Iṭmīnān**

Iṭmīnān plays a crucial role in promoting mental health by providing a state of peacefulness. *Iṭmīnān* is achieved through deep faith in Allāh and trust in His Divine plan. This state of inner calm helps individuals navigate the uncertainties of life with a sense of peace, which is supported by psychological research showing that trust in a higher power can reduce anxiety and enhance emotional regulation (Koenig, 2012). When individuals feel assured and content with their circumstances, as one does with *iṭmīnān*, they are less likely to dwell on past mistakes or future anxieties, they remain in the present. This can significantly improve mental health (Kabat-Zinn, 2003).

Conclusion

The powerful interplay between Qur'ânic spiritual concepts and psychological well-being stems from the holistic approach Islām offers to the human experience. These concepts guide individuals towards realising their potential as a servant of Allāh by promoting a Tawḥīd -centric worldview. A worldview that helps a believer see life beyond this world, reminding them that an afterlife exists. However, this does not happen at the cost of sacrificing happiness in this life. Islām provides tools to facilitate spiritual and psychological growth to create resilient human beings with overall well-being, including better mental health.

Such growth and resilience are achieved by encouraging a stronger connection with Allāh through *ikhlāṣ* (sincerity), *tawakkul* (trust in Allāh), *du'ā'* (supplication), *dhikr* (remembrance of Allāh), and *tafakkur* (reflection). Hardships are part of this journey necessitating *ṣabr* (patience), *shukr* (gratitude), and *istiqāmah* (steadfastness). None of this is possible without showing humility through *tawbah* (repentance) and *istighfār* (seeking forgiveness). But it all becomes worth it as one is elated through experiences of *riḍā* (contentment), *sakīna* (serenity), and *iṭmīnān* (peacefulness).

References

Abī Dāwūd. In-book reference: Book 8, Hadith 103. English translation: Book 8, Hadith 1513. https://sunnah.com/abudawud:1518.

Al-Qushayrī, A. a.-Q. (2007). *Al-Qushayrī's epistle on Sufism* (A. Knysh, Trans.). Garnet Publishing.

Brown, K. W., & Ryan, R. M. (2003). The benefits of being present: Mindfulness and its role in psychological well-being. *Journal of Personality and Social Psychology*, *84*(4), 822–848.

Bukhârî. In-book reference: Book 80, Hadith 4. English translation: Vol. 8, Book 75, Hadith 319. https://sunnah.com/bukhari:6307.

Bybee, J., & Quiles, Z. N. (1998). Guilt and mental health. In J. Bybee (Ed.), *Guilt and children* (pp. 269–291). Academic Press.

Hölzel, B. K., Lazar, S. W., Gard, T., Schuman-Olivier, Z., Vago, D. R., & Ott, U. (2011). How does mindfulness meditation work? Proposing mechanisms of action from a conceptual and neural perspective. *Perspectives on Psychological Science*, *6*(6), 537–559.

Ibn ʻAbbās. (2008). *Tafsīr Ibn ʻAbbās [Tafsīr of Ibn ʻAbbās]* (M. Gezzou, Trans.). Fons Vitae.

Ibn Mājah. In-book reference: Book 37, Hadith 151. English translation: Vol. 5, Book 37, Hadith 4250. https://sunnah.com/ibnmajah:4250.

Kabat-Zinn, J. (2003). Mindfulness-based interventions in context: Past, present, and future. *Clinical Psychology: Science and Practice*, *10*(2), 144–156.

Khalil, A. (2014). Contentment, satisfaction and good-pleasure: Rida in early Sufi moral psychology. *Studies in Religion/Sciences Religieuses*, *43*(3), 371–389.

Koenig, H. G. (2012). Religion, spirituality, and health: The research and clinical implications. *ISRN Psychiatry*, 2012, 1–33.

Maḥallī, J. D., & al-Suyūṭī, J. D. (2007). *Tafsīr al-Jalālayn [Tafsīr of the two Jalāls]* (A. Bewley, Trans.). Dar Al Taqwa.

Muslim (a). In-book reference: Book 50, Hadith 13. English translation: Book 37, Hadith 6622. https://sunnah.com/muslim:2749.

Muslim (b). In-book reference: Book 50, Hadith 4. English translation: Book 37, Hadith 6613. https://sunnah.com/muslim:2749.

Rothman, A. (2018). An Islamic theoretical orientation to psychotherapy. In C. York Al-Karam (Ed.), *Islamically integrated psychotherapy: Uniting faith and professional practice* (pp. 25–56). Templeton Press.

Schimmel, A., & Ernst, C. W. (2011). *Mystical dimensions of Islam*. University of North Carolina Press.

Sheldon, K. M., & Lyubomirsky, S. (2007). Is it possible to become happier? (And if so, how?). *Social and Personality Psychology Compass*, *1*(1), 129–145.

Tangney, J. P., Boone, A. L., & Dearing, R. (2007). Forgiving the self: Conceptual issues and empirical findings. In E. L. Worthington Jr. (Ed.), *Handbook of forgiveness* (pp. 143–158). Routledge.

Tirmidhî (a). In-book reference: Book 37, Hadith 85. English translation: Vol. 4, Book 11, Hadith 2499. https://sunnah.com/muslim:2744a.

Tirmidhî (b). In-book reference: Book 48, Hadith 168. English translation: Vol. 6, Book 45, Hadith 3537. https://sunnah.com/tirmidhi/48.

Worthington, E. L., & Wade, N. G. (Eds.). (2020). *Handbook of forgiveness* (Second edition). Routledge.

9 Conclusion

Summary

Islāmic psychology is deeply rooted in the Qur'ânic worldview, providing a comprehensive understanding of human nature by integrating spiritual, mental, emotional, physical, and social dimensions. Through this approach, Islāmic psychology offers a holistic approach that combines spiritual teachings that positively impact mental and emotional well-being. It views spirituality as an essential part of psychological health, with the state of a person's connection with Allāh directly affecting their mental and emotional well-being. The framework of Islāmic psychology goes beyond focusing on mental states and emphasises the complete individual, as described in the Qur'ân and *ḥadīth*.

The core themes of Islāmic psychology, as discussed in this book, interweave Qur'ânic perspectives on human faculties, Islāmic practices, and spiritual concepts. These elements provide a foundation for understanding how the Qur'ân addresses human behaviour, thought, and spiritual principles that contribute to human flourishing and mental well-being.

Central to this approach, the human faculties, *rūḥ* (spirit), *qalb* (heart), *'aql* (intellect), and *nafs* (self), work together to fulfil the purpose of worshipping Allāh, an inclination which is embedded within the *fiṭrah*.

The *fiṭrah*, or innate nature, is like the spiritual DNA of a person. It inclines individuals towards believing in and adhering to the religion of Islām. The *rūḥ*, or the spirit, is a means to connect with Allāh. The *qalb*, or heart, is not just a physical organ but also a spiritual centre with its fundamental purpose being to believe in Allāh. The 'aql, or intellect, is the tool for thinking and understanding, which enables believers to know Allāh. The *nafs*, or self, facilitates a believer to relate to Allāh as it goes through a journey of purification.

The five pillars of Islām serve as essential acts of worship that guide every facet of a Muslim's life. They form a comprehensive framework that fosters a deep connection with Allāh, promoting personal development, self-discipline, and emotional resilience. By engaging in these practices, Muslims are not only working towards their spiritual growth but also improving their mental well-being while contributing to a more just and cohesive society. Each pillar

DOI: 10.4324/9781003494614-9

facilitates detachments from worldly matters, which can be an obstacle to a strong connection with Allāh. Ultimately, the five pillars represent the foundation of a balanced and fulfilling life in this world, while preparing believers for the eternal rewards of the afterlife.

Qur'ânic spiritual concepts guide individuals towards realising their potential as a servant of Allāh by promoting a *Tawḥīd*-centric worldview. A worldview that helps a believer see life beyond this world, reminding them that an afterlife exists. However, this does not happen at the cost of sacrificing happiness in this life. Islām provides tools to facilitate spiritual and psychological growth to create resilient human beings with overall well-being, including better mental health.

Such growth and resilience are achieved by encouraging a stronger connection with Allāh through *ikhlāṣ* (sincerity), *tawakkul* (trust in Allāh), *du'ā'* (supplication), *dhikr* (remembrance of Allāh), and *tafakkur* (reflection). Hardships are part of this journey necessitating *ṣabr* (patience), *shukr* (gratitude), and *istiqāmah* (steadfastness). None of this is possible without showing humility through *tawbah* (repentance) and *istighfār* (seeking forgiveness). But it all becomes worth it as one is elated through experiences of *riḍā* (contentment), *sakīna* (serenity), and *iṭmīnān* (peacefulness).

Overall, the Qur'ânic teachings discussed in this book offer a comprehensive framework for achieving psychological well-being through the acknowledgement that spirituality and mental health are deeply intertwined. Qur'ânic teachings encourage psychological well-being that is grounded in faith. Through the integration of spiritual, mental, emotional, social, and physical dimensions, Islāmic psychology offers a holistic approach for individuals to flourish.

Index

FSC
www.fsc.org
MIX
Papier | Fördert
gute Waldnutzung
FSC® C083411

Kolibri 360 GmbH
Ferdinand-Jühlke-Straße 7
99095 Erfurt, Deutschland
produktsicherheit@kolibri360.de